THE
CITIES
BOOK

THE CITIES BOOK

Published in September 2016
by Lonely Planet Global Ltd.
CRN 554153
ISBN 978 1 78657 018 5
www.lonelyplanetkids.com
© Lonely Planet 2016

10 9 8 7 6 5 4 3 2 1

Printed in Italy

Produced for Lonely Planet Kids by 38a The Shop

Publishing Director Piers Pickard
Publisher Tim Cook
Commissioning Editor Jen Feroze
Designer Andy Mansfield
Illustrators Livi Gosling and Tom Woolley
Authors Heather Carswell, Bridget Gleeson, Patrick Kinsella,
Hugh McNaughtan, Nicola Williams, Karla Zimmerman
Print production Larissa Frost and Nigel Longuet

Thanks to Joe Bindloss, Laura Crawford, Megan Eaves, Helen Elfer, Gemma
Graham, Alexander Howard, Bailey Johnson, Flora McQueen, Ma Sovaida
Morgan, Matt Phillips, James Smart, Anna Tyler, Branislava Vladisavljevic,
Tasmin Waby, Rebecca Warren, Clifton Wilkinson.

LONELY PLANET OFFICES

Australia
The Malt Store, Level 3, 551 Swanston Street, Carlton 3053,
Victoria, Australia
Phone 03 8379 8000
Email talk2us@lonelyplanet.com.au

USA
150 Linden St, Oakland, CA 94607
Phone 510 250 6400
Email info@lonelyplanet.com

UK
240 Blackfriars Road, London SE1 8NW
Email go@lonelyplanet.co.uk

MIX
Paper from
responsible sources
FSC™ C021741

Paper in this book is certified against the
Forest Stewardship Council™ standards.
FSC™ promotes environmentally responsible, socially beneficial and economically
viable management of the world's forests.

THE
CITIES
BOOK

Illustrated by
Livi Gosling and Tom Woolley

CONTENTS

N

W   E

S

The world is full of fascinating cities! Put your finger on the map and pick one out. The dotted line will lead you to the right page number for the city. You can explore whole continents or jump from place to place – the choice is up to you.

STOCKHOLM
66-67

BERLIN
86-87

EUROPE

MOSCOW
96-99

PYONGYANG
182-183

MUNICH
88-89

ULAANBAATAR
158-159

PRAGUE
92-93

PRIPYAT
100-101

SEOUL
184-185

BĚIJĪNG
160-163

KRAKÓW
90-91

SAMARKAND
150-151

ISTANBUL
102-105

TOKYO
176-179

VIENNA
94-95

ASIA

CHÉNGDŪ
164-165

ATHENS
106-107

JERUSALEM
142-145

KYOTO
180-181

ROME 108-109

THIMPHU
156-157

DUBAI
148-149

HANOI
172-173

HONG KONG
166-167

CAIRO
124-127

MECCA
146-147

ADDIS ABABA
132-133

MANILA
174-175

SOUTH TARAWA
208-209

AFRICA

MUMBAI
152-153

NAIROBI
134-135

VARANASI
154-155

BANGKOK
168-169

DARWIN
186-187

APIA
206-207

ZANZIBAR TOWN
136-137

SINGAPORE
170-171

OCEANIA

PERTH
188-189

AUCKLAND
198-199

SYDNEY
194-197

BALLARAT
190-191

MELBOURNE
192-193

ROTORUA
200-201

The index is on page 210.

QUEENSTOWN
202-205

Turn to page 167 to find out about life in the gleaming skyscrapers of Hong Kong.

Explore the flamboyant *favelas* of Rio de Janeiro on page 52.

IN WHICH CITY COULD YOU DISCOVER...

The bones of a fire-breathing dragon?
Page 90.

Castles made out of human building blocks?
Page 119.

Market stalls selling roasted rodents?
Page 57.

Space-age babies climbing up a tower?
Page 93.

People bathing in mud from an active volcano?
Page 201.

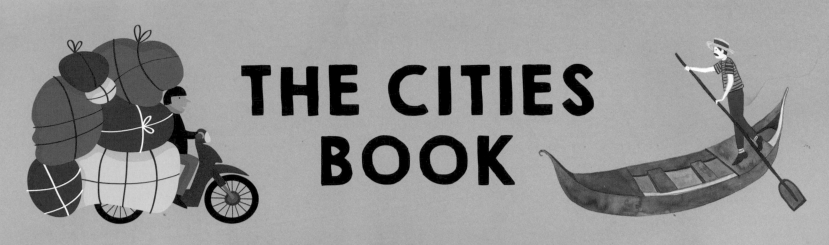

THE CITIES BOOK

You probably think you know what a city is. It's a place where lots of people live – like a town, only bigger. You even might live in a big city yourself, and be tempted to think that all of them are the same. This book is going to blow your mind.

Around the world people come together to live, work and play in thousands of exciting and extraordinary locations. Each time, the geography of the land combines with the culture and history of its people to create a city that is as incredible as it is unique.

In the pages of this book you'll discover cities filled with sand-swept mud houses, beautiful felt yurts, ancient stone buildings and eye-popping modern architecture. Some have canals instead of streets, others cling to snowy mountain peaks while some are lapped by ocean waves. Find out about daily life for the people that live there – their clothes, the food they eat, their festivals and the sports they love to play.

Are you ready to get up and go?
The ultimate city break starts now!

LOOK OUT FOR THE LOCATOR

At the start of each new city page, you'll find a handy locator map. It pinpoints where the city sits within its country, but also where it is placed in the world. Each continent is shown in a different colour. The introduction underneath will give you a flavour of the city before you dive down into its streets.

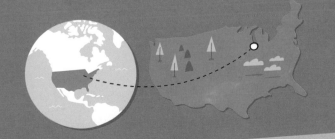

TORONTO
CANADA North America

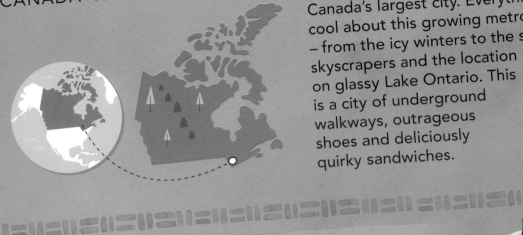

With a population of over six million, Toronto is by far and away Canada's largest city. Everything's cool about this growing metropolis – from the icy winters to the silvery skyscrapers and the location on glassy Lake Ontario. This is a city of underground walkways, outrageous shoes and deliciously quirky sandwiches.

ISLAND STYLE

The Toronto Islands are a chain of tiny islands scattered offshore from the city in Lake Ontario. People have lovely homes there, but cars are not permitted. Instead, everyone gets around by boat or bicycle. Or they walk under the water. The city recently built a pedestrian tunnel that stretches from the islands' airport to the mainland, diving 30 metres (98 feet) beneath the waves.

HOCKEY MANIA!

Ice hockey is Canada's national winter sport. Children start ice skating lessons as young as two and by the age of five are playing in hockey leagues. If they're good enough, they might one day be honoured in the Hockey Hall of Fame. It's one of Toronto's most popular museums – a grand building stuffed full of hockey paraphernalia.

WHOOPEE DOO

Toronto has invented lots of great things including insulin and anti-gravity suits, but nothing beats the whoopee cushion. The noisy pink bags are sold in joke shops all across the world. In the 1930s, employees at the JEM Rubber Company were playing around with scrap sheets of rubber when they discovered the funny sound they could make. Next time you plop down on a whoopee cushion and a big, bubbly bottom sound blows forth, thank Toronto for the laugh!

THE BIG SHOEBOX

The building in Toronto that looks like a giant shoebox holds lots and lots of… shoes! The Bata Shoe Museum has a collection of 13,000 pairs. There are sealskin boots, clown shoes, space boots, fairy princess slippers and even the Dalai Lama's flip-flops!

LIFE BENEATH THE EARTH

Winters in the city are so cold, Toronto has built a system of underground walkways to help residents get around while avoiding the sub-zero temperatures. Thirty kilometres (19 miles) of paths connect up City Hall, museums, hotels and countless office buildings. It's possible to get nearly everywhere without coming to the surface.

FAVOURITE SANDWICH

The peameal bacon sandwich is a Toronto specialty. Never heard of peameal? It's a tasty mix of ground yellow peas. In the late 1800s this was used to help preserve meat – a peameal bacon sandwich was made of slices of pork rolled in peameal, grilled and then heaped onto a bun. Cornmeal is used instead of peameal these days. On a busy Saturday, the Carousel Bakery in St Lawrence Market can expect to sell over 2,600 peameal sandwiches in a single day.

A WALK IN THE CLOUDS

You can't miss the big needle poking up above Toronto's soaring skyline. The CN Tower is the Western Hemisphere's tallest freestanding structure, rising 553.3m (1,815ft) into the air. Glass elevators whisk you to the top and on a clear day you can see as far as Niagara Falls. Daredevils can strap into a harness, join a tour and walk the perimeter. Just don't look down!

PEOPLE FROM EVERYWHERE

Toronto is said to be the most culturally diverse city in the world. Forty-nine per cent of its residents were born in a different country, and more than 140 languages are spoken. Ethnic neighbourhoods pop up everywhere. As well as Little Portugal, there's Little Italy, Little India, Little Tibet, Little Jamaica – and that's just the 'littles'! Chinatown, Greektown and Koreatown are also thriving communities.

MONTRÉAL
CANADA North America

Montréal is very French – residents say *bonjour* more often than 'hello'. It's a sociable metropolis that bustles with people playing in parks, gathering at festivals and meeting in outdoor cafés. As it approaches the ripe old age of 400, Montréal is also one of Canada's oldest cities. Stone forts and fur trading posts hint at its historic past.

PARLEZ-VOUS FRANÇAIS?
French is Montréal's main language. More people speak French here than in any city outside of Paris. You greet friends in Montréal as you would in France – with a light kiss on both cheeks. Plenty of people speak English here too, however. The Boulevard Saint-Laurent is considered the dividing line between French and English speaking Montréal. Most French speakers live east of the street, whilst English speakers reside to the west.

CHILLY CHILDREN
Montréal is an all-year-round outdoor city. When the weather gets cold, children pull on their mittens and trudge to their local park. The city's hills, ponds and trails are transformed into winter wonderlands – perfect for skiing, sledging and building snowmen. Montréal has many winter festivals every year, some of which encourage families to try new activities such as ice sliding and snow scootering.

FIND THE FORT
Settlers from France founded Montréal in 1642. Not long after, they built a fort around the city for protection. If you had visited Montréal in the 18th century, you'd have seen stone walls and gates with drawbridges all around. The Pointe-à-Callière Museum of Archaeology and History still has underground remnants of the walls.

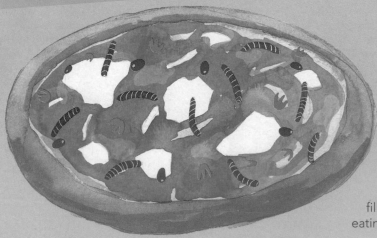

WORM PIZZA
Montréal's Insectarium is one of the world's biggest bug zoos, housing everything from long-horned beetles and hissing cockroaches to furry tarantulas and cobra butterflies. The museum used to host a public insect tasting event each year, when you could eat cricket-stuffed mushrooms, worm-topped pizza and other bug-filled snacks. Tastings still happen every now and then. The word for eating bugs, by the way, is 'entomophagy'.

STUFFED

Montréal has around 6,500 restaurants – more per square kilometre than anywhere in North America. Locals love to eat out, chowing down on smoked meat sandwiches, bagels and *steak frites* (steak and fries). North African eateries serve *couscous* (a rice-like dish with spicy stew ladled on top), and Haitian cafés serve *tassot* (fried goat or beef). The *Montréalais* eat later than in most Canadian and US cities, too. Most eateries don't fill up until at least 9pm.

SUPER SLOPPY SNACK

Locals' favourite snack food is *poutine*. This mound of chips sprinkled with cheese curds and topped with brown gravy certainly looks sloppy, but it tastes gorgeously salty and melty. The snack is so popular it's even sold in McDonald's.

TAM-TAMS JAM

Every Sunday in summer, hundreds of people gather at the George-Étienne Cartier Monument (he was one of Canada's leading statesmen) to join a public drum circle. They arrive with African *djembe* drums, little bongo drums and big bass drums. People also do yoga, walk on tightropes and dress in medieval costumes to joust. The festivities last all day. It's called 'Tam-Tams' after the sounds that the drums make.

MONTRÉAL

Most people don't realise that Montréal is actually an island! The city sits on one of more than 400 islands that float in the St Lawrence River.

A MOUNTAIN MARKS THE SPOT

Montréal's name comes from *Mont Royal*, which means 'Royal Mountain' in French. Mont Royal is more of a big hill than a mountain, but it is the highest point in the city. It's part of a beautiful park where everyone jogs and cycles in summer, then goes sledging and skiing in winter. The giant cross on top of the hill is like the one placed there by Montréal's founder, Paul Chomedey de Maisonneuve. The cross was a symbol of thanks to God for sparing the new settlement from a flood.

BIG BELL

Notre-Dame Basilica is Montréal's most lavish church. It has a midnight-blue ceiling decorated with gold stars, plus the biggest bell in North America. The bell weighs 9,979 kilograms (11 tons) and even has a name – Jean-Baptiste. When Jean-Baptiste tolls it can be heard over 35km (22mi) away. The bell can only be rung on special occasions. It is so large, the vibrations cause damage to the building.

MONT ROYAL

NOTRE-DAME BASILICA

PLACE JACQUES-CARTIER

FAIR AND SQUARE

Place Jacques-Cartier is Montréal's town square. It's where everyone gathers to *prendre un café au lait à la terrasse* – meaning 'drink a coffee with hot milk on a café's outdoor terrace'. People also come to see the street performers who juggle fire, ride unicycles and balance on stacks of tin cans. Every day is like an outdoor carnival.

GROUNDHOG DAY

Montréal's residents share their city streets with a vast array of urban wildlife. Birds wheel overhead, skunks and squirrels pop up in gardens, and raccoons scavenge through dustbins. In June 2015, one plucky groundhog surprised Formula 1 fans by strolling onto the racetrack during the Canadian Grand Prix! Luckily drivers were able to swerve and the critter scampered to safety.

PONT
JACQUES-CARTIER

LOUIS-HIPPOLYTE
LAFONTAINE BRIDGE-TUNNEL

ST LAWRENCE RIVER

LA RONDE

WORLD'S BIGGEST FIREWORKS

The Montréal International Fireworks Festival is the Olympics of fireworks events! Teams from all over the globe compete against each other at La Ronde during the month of July to see who can create the most impressive show. The night sky booms, sizzles and blazes with colour on a scale unmatched anywhere else in the world.

CIRCUIT GILLES
VILLENEUVE

BEAVER HAT CRAZE

In the 1700s and early 1800s, Montréal was a hub for fur trading. Beaver-pelt hats were all the rage in Europe, and companies needed to get furs from the trappers who lived inland to ships that could cross the sea. They hired boatmen called *voyageurs* (travellers) to fetch them. The *voyageurs* paddled canoes for 16 hours a day to forts, traded supplies for pelts, then paddled back to Lachine, a part of Montréal near the port. The fur traders' old warehouse still stands there today.

VANCOUVER
CANADA North America

Many people believe that Vancouver is the prettiest city on the planet, and who's to argue? The mountains meet the sea in grand form, while a rainforest sprouts at downtown's edge. The people here are outdoorsy and laid-back, with a taste for adventurous eating.

TOWERING TOTEM POLES

The Museum of Anthropology holds an awesome collection of totem poles. Carvers from the surrounding First Nations have been making them for centuries. The First Nations are the native people of Canada, who lived here long before Europeans arrived. Each totem pole is a record of a community's or a family's history. The artists sculpt animals – such as the eagle, grizzly bear, orca, frog and raven – into the poles to convey the story. They use red or yellow cedar wood, as it doesn't rot easily. Even so, the typical pole only lasts 100 years before it starts to decay.

URBAN RAINFOREST

Take a short walk from the glass skyscrapers of downtown Vancouver and suddenly you're in the heart of a forest. Stanley Park has a vast spread of cedar, fir and hemlock trees. There are half a million of them, to be exact, with many towering giants boasting centuries of growth. The park is surrounded by sea. Trails take you past harbour seals while bald eagles swoop overhead. It's hard to believe that all this is just a few blocks from the city centre!

SWINGING IN THE TREETOPS

You have to be brave to walk across the Capilano Suspension Bridge. Not only is it one of the longest and highest of its kind, it also sways and bobs as you make your way across. Did we mention it's set way up in the trees, over a racing river in a gorge 70m (230ft) below? The handrails help you stay steady, but fearless types cross without holding on.

WORLD'S GROSSEST GELATO?

Vancouver's famous La Casa Gelato store scoops 218 flavours of Italian-style ice cream. There's chocolate, of course, and fruity licks like pineapple and strawberry. Vanilla gummy bear is delicious, but would you eat garlic or seaweed flavours? Best not to ask about the peanut butter curry and purple yam! Luckily you can try before you buy.

SUSHI, SUSHI AND MORE SUSHI

Sushi is mega popular in Vancouver. Chefs flash long knives to make the dish – sliced fish served with rice and seaweed – at more than 600 sushi restaurants. One out of every ten restaurants here serves sushi.

SAILING SHIPS

Vancouver is Canada's largest port. More than 3,000 cruise ships, oil tankers, fishing boats and vessels glide in and out of the bays every year. Most of the cruise ships head north to Alaska. Most of the cargo ships sail to China, Japan and elsewhere in Asia, carrying wheat, cars and lumber, amongst other goods. Sometimes the ships have company – orcas and other whales share the port's waters.

LONGEST SWIMMING POOL

The neighbourhood of Kitsilano has the longest saltwater pool in North America. The swimming lanes stretch for 137m (450ft) – almost the length of three Olympic pools. Even the greatest Olympic swimmer of all time, Michael Phelps, might be out of breath after freestyling his way from one end to the other!

SAN FRANCISCO
USA North America

San Francisco is sprawled across no less than 43 hills. It's lapped by water on three sides, nestled in a spot that is frequently wreathed in swirling fog. Throw in cable cars, a world famous bridge and a prison island and it's easy to see why this is one of the USA's most fascinating cities.

GOLD RUSH

The discovery of gold in the nearby town of Coloma in 1848 caused men from across the globe to flock to California in search of a slice of the riches. The Gold Rush was over in a few short years, but it changed San Francisco forever. The arrival of money and hordes of people transformed the former fishing village into a world famous city.

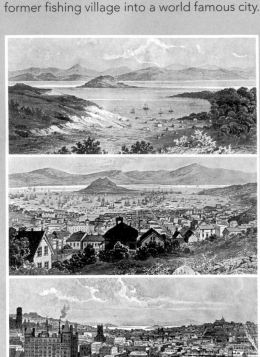

THE GREAT GOLDEN GATE BRIDGE

Stretching 2.7km (1.7mi) across San Francisco Bay, the magnificent Golden Gate Bridge is one of the seven wonders of the modern world. Two huge cables containing over 128,750km (80,000mi) of wire support it – enough to circle the Earth three times over. The bridge's famous deep orange paintwork makes it easier for ships to spot. Despite this, on some days the fog is so thick the bridge can disappear from view completely.

UGLY LAW

The city once had an outrageous rule that stopped people it considered to be unattractive from appearing in public. Nicknamed the 'Ugly Law', those banned from the streets included anyone with an unsightly disability or disease, as well as residents who were maimed or mutilated. The law, which was introduced in 1867, has since been abolished. Today San Francisco is known for its warm and welcoming attitude.

KILLER QUAKES

In 1906 San Francisco was rocked by a terrible earthquake. Around 3,000 people died and over 80 per cent of the city was destroyed. This was the deadliest natural disaster to hit California, but unfortunately it wasn't a one-off. San Francisco is located on a fault line, so another large earthquake could strike at any time.

ISLAND PRISON

For nearly 30 years the small island of Alcatraz in San Francisco Bay was home to one of America's most famous prisons. Nicknamed 'the Rock', the jail was said to be impossible to escape from, although many tried. None of the 36 men who attempted to flee were thought to be successful, however five prisoners are listed as missing. They are believed to have drowned, even though their bodies have never been found…

ON A ROLL

San Franciscans are determined to do all they can to protect their city from earthquakes. All new buildings are now specially constructed so they can withstand tremors. Even the airport was built on large steel ball bearings to allow it to move without collapsing when a quake strikes.

HELP ON THE HILLS

A packed cable car climbing a steep city street is one of San Francisco's most iconic sights. The vehicles were introduced nearly 150 years ago to replace the horse-drawn streetcars, which struggled to travel on the slippery hill roads. The easy hop-on, hop-off system and the way the cars spirit you effortlessly up leg-achingly sharp slopes have made them a much loved part of the city.

LOVABLE LOCALS

Pier 39 is home to some of the city's noisiest residents – hundreds of California sea lions! Arriving at the pier after an earthquake in 1989, the playful creatures were considered a nuisance at first, but soon became a hit with locals and tourists alike.

PIER 39

LOS ANGELES

USA North America

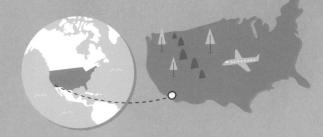

With golden beaches and virtually non-stop sunshine, Los Angeles is just as good looking as its rich and famous residents. As the birthplace of some of the biggest blockbuster movies in history, the city is packed with reminders that it's all about the glittery world of show business.

LA LOOKING GOOD

In an area full of glamorous movie and TV stars it's no surprise that the locals spend a lot of time, effort and money on their appearance. Trendsetting LA doesn't just offer the usual gym classes, beauty treatments and restaurants either. This is a city that loves to spark new trends! Anything goes – from circus-themed workouts to gold and caviar facials, and restaurants that only serve raw food.

DAZZLING DISNEY

The unusual design of the Walt Disney Concert Hall caused people to get hot under the collar when it was first built. The hall's steel, sail-shaped curves reflected so much sunshine that nearby buildings were heated up, and passers-by were blinded by the dazzling glare. The problem was eventually solved by sanding down the shiny metal exterior.

GIVE US A HAND

Another mecca for celeb-spotters on Hollywood Boulevard is the TCL Chinese Theatre, a hot spot for movie premières. Film stars leave their handprints, footprints and autographs in cement on the cinema's forecourt. There are also more unusual prints including the wands from the Harry Potter films.

HISTORIC HOLLYWOOD

The Christie-Nestor Studio, the first movie studio in Hollywood, was set up over 100 years ago. Filmmakers were lured to LA by the range of varied locations around the city and the great weather – Los Angeles made outdoor filming possible all year round. Other studios soon followed and Hollywood quickly became the centre of the American film industry.

HUMONGOUS HOUSES

The homes of LA's rich and famous are some of the most lavish in the world. Those with big bucks live in houses that boast gigantic swimming pools, bowling alleys, cinemas and vineyards. One A-list star's home (complete with basketball courts and private golf course) has become so sprawling, it now has its own postcode!

WALK AMONG THE STARS

On the Hollywood Walk of Fame you can strut along a sidewalk dotted with the names of the showbiz world's top talent. Celebrities are awarded the honour of having a star if they have contributed to one of five entertainment industries – motion pictures, television, music, radio or live performance.

A CITY ON SCREEN

Most Los Angeles residents manage to keep their cool when they spot actors hard at work. With around 100 crews filming on any average day, the sight is nothing out of the ordinary! Once a year, however, movie madness takes over the entire town. Stars work the red carpet at the lavish Academy Awards ceremony, hoping to bag themselves a coveted Oscar statuette.

HOLLYWOOD SIGN

On a hillside overlooking the city, giant white letters – each one is 13.7m (45ft) high – spell out 'HOLLYWOOD'. The beloved sign is the ultimate selfie backdrop for tourists! What many people don't realise is that the sign was originally an advert for new homes that read 'HOLLYWOODLAND'. In 1949, 26 years after the sign was born, 'LAND' was dropped and the sign became forever linked with the movie-making business.

LAS VEGAS
USA North America

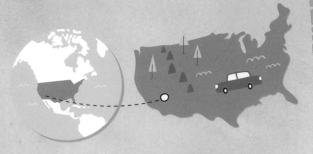

VEGAS BY NUMBERS

Visitors to the city in 2014	41 million
Miles of neon lighted tubing	15,000
Weddings each day	300
Biggest ever slot machine win	$39.7 million
Bedrooms at the MGM Grand	over 5,000
Water jets in the Bellagio Hotel's fountain	1,200

Rising from the desert like a neon oasis, Las Vegas is a jaw-dropping extravaganza. Along the Strip, some of the world's biggest hotels lure people in with their colossal casinos and wacky themes. In this crazy, colourful city you can ride in a Venetian gondola, sleep in a pyramid and get married by the king of rock and roll.

FAMOUS FOUNTAINS

The Bellagio Hotel is one of the Strip's most popular attractions. Its world-famous fountain puts on spectacular displays. High-powered jets send water twirling to music, spinning and dancing as high as 140m (460ft) into the air.

CITY OF LIGHT

Vegas doesn't let a little thing like night-time slow it down! Whether you fancy a late night buffet, want to get married at midnight or gamble until the sun comes up, anything is possible. When viewed from space, the Las Vegas Strip at night is said to be the brightest stretch of land on Earth.

SHOW BUSINESS

The hottest stars on the planet perform in Vegas. From magic to acrobatics, comedy to music, every show shimmers with glitz and glamour. O by Cirque du Soleil features world-class gymnasts, divers and synchronized swimmers performing in and around a pool holding 6.8 million litres (1.5 million gallons) of water.

WEDDING CAPITAL OF THE WORLD

Las Vegas is one of the most famous spots on the planet to get married. Couples can tie the knot with a drive-thru wedding, take a gondola through the Venetian hotel's Grand Canal or get hitched by an Elvis Presley impersonator.

RIDE ON HIGH

The tallest freestanding observation tower in the USA is called the Stratosphere – home to a high altitude theme park. Thrill seekers hop onto rides that catapult them over the edge of the tower, then leave them dangling 109 storeys in the air. For the truly fearless there is also the Sky Jump. Gutsy visitors are lowered at heart-stopping speed all the way to the ground in the highest controlled descent in the world.

STRATOSPHERE

SKIPPING THE STRIP

The Strip creates jobs for a huge number of locals, but in their free-time most city dwellers choose to avoid this tourist hot spot. To escape the desert heat, families head out instead to the surrounding canyons and mountains. There's fun to be had hiking, biking, kayaking and, in winter, even skiing.

CAESARS PALACE

BONKERS BUFFETS

In a city where biggest, brashest and brightest rule, it's no surprise that the eating options are equally over the top. Caesars Palace is home to one of the city's largest buffets with 500 dishes to choose from every single day.

THE VENETIAN

PARIS

FRENCH FANCY

When it comes to themed venues, Las Vegas goes all out! The Paris Hotel is entirely based on the French capital, featuring a half-sized replica of the Eiffel Tower outside with its own observation deck and restaurant. Visitors strolling through the cobbled boulevards inside the hotel can gaze up at other landmarks, including the Louvre and the Paris Opera House.

BELLAGIO

MGM GRAND

PYRAMID OF LIGHT

At the Egyptian themed Luxor Hotel, guests stay in a 30-storey high pyramid made out of black glass. At night the tip of the pyramid projects a ray of light into the sky above the city. The beam is so brilliant it can be seen by airline pilots 160km (100mi) away.

LUXOR HOTEL

A GRAND PLACE TO STAY

In a city packed with places to stay, the MGM Grand takes the crown. With 20 vast restaurants, 5 swimming pools and a wedding chapel, it is one of the largest hotels on Earth.

NEW ORLEANS
USA North America

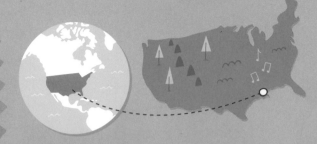

New Orleans is a city that loves to have fun. Festivals turn the streets into richly coloured, raucous parties, the scent of spicy seafood soups and stews fill the air, and, in the birthplace of jazz, you're rarely out of earshot of thumping live music.

A BITE TO EAT

Diners in New Orleans can sink their teeth into something a little different for lunch by snapping up a plate of alligator. The delicacy can be found in a variety of dishes in restaurants throughout the city, ranging from gator sausages to alligator cheesecake. Louisiana has a large alligator population, with between 1.5 and 2 million in the wild and hundreds of thousands more on alligator farms. It's no surprise that the giant reptiles have crept onto menus to sit alongside local dishes like rice-based *jambalaya* and *gumbo*, a seafood filled stew.

VOODOO QUEEN

In the 19th century New Orleans was under the spell of voodoo queen, Marie Laveau, who introduced many in the city to the mysterious religion. Voodoo followers believe that the living world exists alongside the invisible world of the dead, filled with spirits who watch over and inspire us. Stories of dancing wildly around bonfires have become legendary, but Marie is also credited with helping the poor and needy with her practices. Today her influence can still be felt round the city – there are voodoo shops, voodoo tours and even a voodoo festival.

SUPER BRIDGE

The Lake Pontchartrain Causeway is the world's longest continuous bridge over water, spanning an incredible 38.41km (23.87mi). It's a breathtaking way to enter the city! Made of two parallel bridges, the causeway carves a direct route from Mandeville in the north to the suburbs of New Orleans in the south.

FRENCH QUARTER

The oldest neighbourhood in the city is the French Quarter. As New Orleans was founded by the French, and for a while ruled by the Spanish, this historic part of the city is a beautiful blend of styles. The area is famous for its balconied buildings and is a hotspot for tourists who can enjoy mule-drawn carriage rides, street performers, museums and lively nightlife.

ALL THE FUN OF THE FESTIVAL

New Orleans puts on a whopping 130 festivals a year, which works out as roughly one every three days. The annual Mardi Gras is the biggest event, but there are all sorts of dazzling and unusual parades. One highlight is a procession of dogs dressed up in weird and wacky outfits!

HURRICANE KATRINA

On the morning of 29 August 2005 a lethal storm hit Louisiana. Hurricane Katrina spiralled into New Orleans, bringing heavy rain and winds of 200 kilometres per hour (125 miles per hour), but it was the overflowing waters that followed which caused the greatest devastation. The floods turned Katrina into one of the deadliest storms ever to strike the United States.

Hurricane Katrina devastated much of the coastal region of Mississippi and southeastern Louisiana, but New Orleans was the largest city affected by the storm. The city was in a vulnerable position, not only did it lie below sea level, but it was also surrounded by water on three sides – Lake Pontchartrain, the Mississippi River and marshland. The hurricane caused a surge in water levels that breached the city's flood defences, leaving the people of New Orleans scrambling onto rooftops to escape. Two days after the storm hit, 80 per cent of the city was underwater.

While most of the city was evacuated, many people couldn't get away in time. Over 25,000 residents sought shelter in the Louisiana Superdome. With the city destroyed, and food and fresh water in short supply, people began to loot homes and businesses. The National Guard were finally brought in to restore law and order.

Over 1,800 people died as a result of Hurricane Katrina and one million were left homeless. It was also the costliest natural disaster in US history, with more than 100 billion dollars of damage caused by the catastrophic storm.

Appalled by the scale of destruction and suffering, the world dug deep. Money, specialist equipment and workers were all donated to the relief campaign. The city has taken a long time to bounce back, but now, with homes rebuilt and stronger flood defences in place, it is looking forward to a bright future.

NASHVILLE

USA   North America

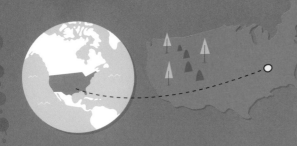

Guitars twang and neon lights blaze in Nashville. Country music is the city's main business, but tunes of all kinds fill the air. It's a polite city – and Tennessee's capital – with a southern accent and taste for hot chicken and gooey chocolate treats.

WHERE COUNTRY BEGAN

In 1925, a Nashville radio host invited fiddle and banjo players to come to the studio to perform bluegrass or 'country' music from the nearby Appalachian Mountains. People across America heard it, and that's how country music became famous. The radio show was called the Grand Ole Opry and it's still on every Friday and Saturday night in more than 30 US states. Now it broadcasts from the Grand Ole Opry House, a 4,372-seat theatre where country music's top stars perform.

GOOEY TREATS

Nashville has its own candy bar called the Goo Goo Cluster – a sticky blend of marshmallow, peanuts and caramel wrapped in milk chocolate. A local factory started making the treat more than 100 years ago, and now 20,000 Goo Goos an hour pop out of the plant. No one is sure how the candy got its name, although some say it comes from the first words that a baby says.

CHRISTMAS IN JULY

Nashville's Opryland Hotel is one of the world's most enormous hotels. It's so big that a river runs through it! There's a mansion built inside its glass walls, along with 17 restaurants and 2,882 rooms. Staff start decorating for Christmas in July – it takes months to string two million lights up through the hotel's trees.

REVENGE OF THE HOT CHICKEN

Nashville's most famous dish is hot chicken – fried poultry pieces coated in a super-spicy sauce made with cayenne pepper. A local woman invented the recipe to get revenge on her boyfriend. He stayed out too late one night, so she secretly poured loads of hot sauce on his chicken to teach him a lesson the next morning. Turns out he loved it, and started making the peppery recipe at his restaurant soon after. Today eateries all over town fry up hot chicken.

THE OTHER PARTHENON

Have you heard of the Parthenon – the temple built in Greece 2,500 years ago? Nashville has the world's only full-scale replica, and it's much easier to get to! Climb the steps, go through the towering columns, and you'll see the biggest indoor statue in the Western Hemisphere – a gold Athena, the goddess of wisdom. The replica was all built when Nashville held the Tennessee Centennial Exposition (a sort of mini World's Fair) in 1897.

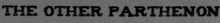

GUITAR-SHAPED DRIVEWAY

Andrew Jackson, the USA's seventh president, lived in Nashville. He's famous for fighting duels and being a war hero (his soldiers nicknamed him 'Old Hickory', because he was as tough as hickory wood), but also for having slaves and forcing Native Americans off their land. His Nashville mansion is called the Hermitage. Weirdly, he built his driveway in the shape of a guitar – and that was in the 1830s, before Nashville became Music City! Many locals think it was an omen.

SINGING AND SONGWRITING

Over the years, so many musicians came to town to play for the Grand Ole Opry that an entire industry grew up around them. Recording studios, record companies and performance halls opened, many packed into an area known as Music Row. Singers and songwriters continue to stream into Nashville to find fame, not just in country music, but in rock, folk and blues, too. No wonder it's nicknamed 'Music City'.

CHICAGO
USA North America

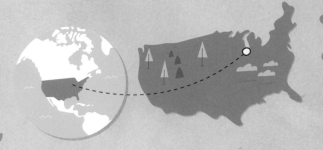

Chicago is tall – some of the world's mightiest skyscrapers rise up here. It's also beach-y, museum-y and inventive, with a backward-flowing river and trains that run on stilts. Lively and competitive by nature, the locals in this city take their sport and their pizza seriously.

CLOUD GATE

One of Chicago's most popular sights is the *Cloud Gate* sculpture by artist Anish Kapoor in Millennium Park. Everybody calls it the 'Bean' and it's not hard to guess why. Visitors are allowed to walk up and touch its shiny, reflective surface, even though they are bound to leave fingerprints. City workers buff the Bean daily with a cloth and spritz it twice a year with a detergent spray to help keep it gleaming.

WINDY CITY?

Despite its 'Windy City' nickname, Chicago isn't especially gusty. The name came about in the 1890s when a New York newspaper described Chicago as 'windy' because of the hot air its politicians spouted to try and win the bid to host the 1893 World's Columbian Exposition.

THE FIRST SKYSCRAPER

Chicago built its first skyscraper in 1885, changing the way modern cities look forever. The Willis Tower remained the tallest building in America until One World Trade Center was built in New York in 2013 and it's still higher than most buildings on Earth. The best way to experience such dizzy heights is to go up to the 103rd floor Skydeck. The deck has glass ledges that jut out from the tower, creating a crazy-scary view down to the ground.

THE GOAT-CURSED BASEBALL TEAM

Built in 1914, Wrigley Field is one of the few old ballparks left. Its home team – the Chicago Cubs – suffers from the longest championship losing streak in US sports history. The unlucky side haven't won a World Series since 1908! The record is said to be the result of a curse. In 1945, a fan called Billy Sianis tried to enter the ballpark with his goat, Murphy, hoping that the pet would be a lucky mascot. When the goat was denied entry, Sianis called a terrible curse down upon the baseball team. Unfortunately it seems to have stuck.

HEAPS OF BEACHES

Chicago's entire eastern border is made up of 26 beaches lapped by vast Lake Michigan. You can swim, kayak and build sandcastles, but unfortunately the water remains icy cold most of the year.

SOLE SURVIVOR

No one knows how the Great Chicago Fire of 1871 started. Tales have been swapped about a cow kicking over a lantern, or a meteor shower sparking the blaze. One thing's for sure – the fire burned for three days and destroyed everything downtown apart from the water tower. Its yellow limestone bricks managed to withstand the flames.

BIG IDEAS

The Ferris wheel was invented in Chicago – there's a replica of the original on Navy Pier. Pinball machines, brownies, zips and deep-dish pizza are also Chicago inventions. To top this, the city created the world's first mobile phone in 1973. It was the size of a brick and went on sale to the public in 1984.

BACKWARD-FLOWING RIVER

The Chicago River is the only one in the world to flow backwards. Engineers reversed the current in 1900 using a series of canals and locks. The goal was to send sewage away from Lake Michigan, where the city got its drinking water. The Chicago is also the only river dyed green every St Patrick's Day.

TRAINS ON STILTS

In 1892, Chicago's streets were unpaved and clogged up with wagons, carts and streetcars. As a solution, planners built a rail system that ran above the messy roads, supported on hundreds of steel stilts. The elevated trains still clatter along the tracks today and the 'L', as it is called, remains the city's main mode of public transport.

WORLD'S LARGEST T. REX

The world's largest *Tyrannosaurus rex* is named Sue, and her 67-million-year-old skeleton guards the Field Museum of Natural History. She's so huge that her bones alone weigh around 1,800 kilograms (4,000 pounds).

NEW YORK

USA North America

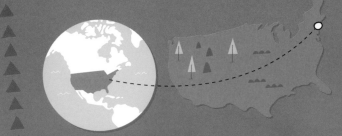

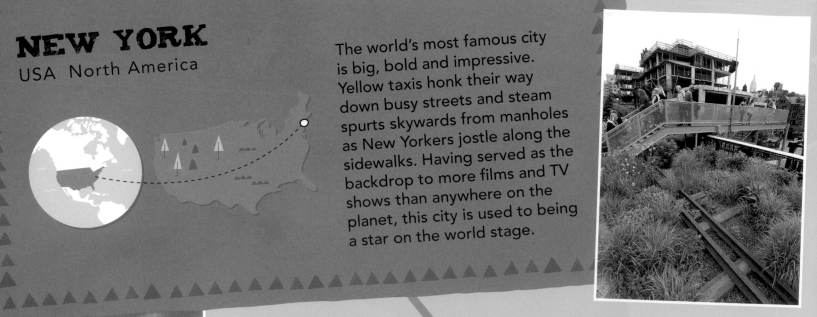

The world's most famous city is big, bold and impressive. Yellow taxis honk their way down busy streets and steam spurts skywards from manholes as New Yorkers jostle along the sidewalks. Having served as the backdrop to more films and TV shows than anywhere on the planet, this city is used to being a star on the world stage.

ONE WORLD TRADE CENTER

The One World Trade Center towers above the rest of the New York skyline. The Western Hemisphere's tallest building was deliberately constructed at a height of 1,776ft (541m). The measurement marks the year 1776, when the United States Declaration of Independence was signed. The 104 floor high super-skyscraper is next to the site of the original World Trade Center whose twin towers were destroyed in a terrorist attack on September 11, 2001. The site is now home to a memorial and museum where visitors can pay their respects to the many people who lost their lives.

WALK THE HIGH LINE

A favourite spot of New Yorkers is the High Line, a park built on a disused railway and elevated above the streets of Manhattan's West Side. The park provides a habitat for wildlife and is used by locals for everything from stargazing to practising tai chi.

ONE WORLD TRADE CENTER

BROOKLYN BRIDGE

STATUE OF LIBERTY

STATUE OF LIBERTY

Lady Liberty is so enormous, she wears size 879 shoes and has a 10.7m (35ft) waistline! Located on Liberty Island, the statue has a narrow staircase inside so that visitors can climb all the way to the crown and take in fantastic views of the city.

GOVERNORS ISLAND

A BIRD'S EYE VIEW

The Brooklyn Bridge, which connects the boroughs of Manhattan and Brooklyn, is not only popular with the thousands of people who cross it every day, it is also a hot spot for peregrine falcons. The rare birds have been found nesting there because it gives them a great view from which to hunt prey. The falcons dive-bomb from their vantage point at speeds of up to 320kph (200mph).

CENTRAL PARK

In a city full of skyscraper-shaded streets, sometimes the sun can barely hit the sidewalk. Central Park provides a much needed escape from the concrete jungle. The park is vast, with 93km (58mi) of paths winding through lawns, trees and lakes. There is even a castle, reservoir and a zoo nestled amongst the greenery.

CENTRAL PARK

THE HIGH LINE

EMPIRE STATE BUILDING

ROCKEFELLER CENTER

FLATIRON BUILDING

NARROW POINT

The Flatiron Building, which takes its name from its unusual triangular shape, is one of the most photographed sights in the city. At the narrow end the rooms inside the building are just under 2m (6.5ft) wide!

LIGHTNING STRIKES

One of the world's most famous landmarks, the Empire State Building, is so tall it gets struck by lightning an average of 23 times per year! Luckily the skyscraper has been fitted with a lightning rod so that there's no chance of anyone coming to harm during stormy weather.

ROCKING AROUND THE CHRISTMAS TREE

New Yorkers love Christmas! The perfect place to get into the festive spirit is the Rockefeller Center, home to the city's most iconic Christmas tree. Every year a twinkling tree up to 30m (100ft) tall is given pride of place in the plaza, overlooking the ice rink.

NEW YORK

Whether you want to chow down in Chinatown, nibble pizza in Little Italy or sample the cuisine of nations from Albania to Yemen, in New York City your taste buds can truly tour the world!

TOM'S DINER

EAT

FEELING PECKISH?

In the Big Apple, the dining options are endless. Food is enjoyed on-the-go from street carts, in cheap and cheerful diners and at the tables of the country's fanciest restaurants.

BRILLIANT BAGELS

New York bagels are said to be the best in the world. The chewy, doughy delights come in a variety of flavours and are traditionally served with a *schmear* (a small spread) of cream cheese. Though no one knows for sure what makes them more delicious than the rest of the planet's offerings, theories range from the blend of ingredients to the time the dough is given to rest before being cooked. It is also believed the city's water – which the bagels are flash boiled in before being baked to perfection – may be key to their success.

HOME OF THE HOT DOG

Hot dogs are a New York staple. Served with *sauerkraut* (a German dish of chopped pickled cabbage), onion sauce or mustard from carts and stands dotted around the city's bustling streets, they make a quick and easy lunch for busy New Yorkers. Dogs are such big business, licences for a cart in the city's most popular spots can cost hundreds of thousands of dollars a year. That's a lot of hot dogs just to cover the rent on your patch!

SWEET SIDE OF THE CITY

New York cheesecake is one of America's ultimate desserts. The smooth and creamy pudding remains a favourite in a city offering a never-ending choice of tasty treats. To stand out from the crowd, chefs and bakers compete to invent new and exciting dishes such as the *cronut* – a delicious doughnut-croissant hybrid.

NATHAN'S HOT DOG EATING CONTEST

A famous food highlight in the New York calendar is the annual Nathan's Hot Dog Eating Contest. The competition, which is held on Coney Island, sees participants wolfing down as many dogs as they can in ten minutes. The 2015 winner managed a stomach-stretching 62 hot dogs!

QUEEN OF THE WORLD

The borough of Queens is one of the city's most diverse areas. Its global vibe means some of the world's more unusual dishes can be found here. New Yorkers with a taste for the exotic can tuck into everything from roast guinea pig in one of the borough's South American restaurants to the wriggly Korean delicacy of live octopus.

PHILADELPHIA
USA North America

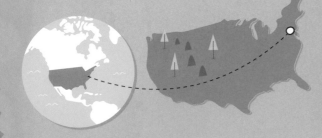

Proud Philadelphia is where some of the most important events in America's history took place. This is where the country was born, where the laws of the land were set and where many of the freedoms that the country enjoys today began. Philadelphia feels noble and clever, and with such a remarkable past it is easy to see why.

ZOO WITH A VIEW
America's oldest zoo likes to keep up with the times! Philadelphia Zoo has a unique animal exploration system that allows creatures to roam around the park. Apes travel from treetop to treetop, while tigers pad along see-through mesh trails and look down on the humans below.

GHOULS AND GANGSTERS
The city's Eastern State Penitentiary is said to be one of the most haunted buildings in the state of Pennsylvania. Since the 1940s, prison guards and inmates have reported spooky sightings and weird experiences. The prison closed in 1971, but that hasn't stopped the ghostly goings-on. Brave visitors can explore the crumbling cells and empty guard towers of the former prison, which was home to some of America's biggest criminals, including the gangster Al Capone.

MAGIC GARDENS
One of the city's most colourful and unusual spots is Philadelphia's Magic Gardens. The sprawling space is a labyrinth of mosaics made up of mirrors, pots, glass, bicycle wheels and lots more. The awesome art is the work of one man, Isaiah Zagar, who started the project to brighten up a rundown area of the city.

MEDICAL MARVELS
The Mütter Museum is home to a huge collection of amazing and abnormal human body parts. With scores of skulls, the brain of famous physicist Albert Einstein and a display of diseased organs, this is not a museum for the faint-hearted!

FIGHTING FOR FREEDOM

In 1775, war broke out between Great Britain and 13 of its North American colonies. The colonies wanted to be free from British rule, but Great Britain fought to keep them under its control. The following year leaders from each of the colonies signed the Declaration of Independence in Philadelphia's Independence Hall. The signing marks the critical moment when the colonies became free states and no longer part of the British Empire. In 1783, the war ended and the United States of America and Great Britain agreed to live in peace.

THE LAND

Another important event in America's history took place in Philadelphia's Independence Hall a few years later, with the signing of the United States Constitution. The Constitution set out the rights of all American citizens and the laws which they must live by. Written and signed in 1787, it continues to be the law of the land today.

LIBERTY BELL

Philadelphia is home to the Liberty Bell, which was famously rung when America became free from British control. The hefty, metal bell weighs over 900kg (2,000lb) and has become a symbol of freedom in the country. No wonder city dwellers were outraged when Mexican food chain Taco Bell bought it and announced that they wanted to rename it the 'Taco Liberty Bell'! Their anger didn't last long however, as it was soon revealed to be an April Fool's joke.

INDEPENDENCE DAY

The anniversary of the signing is known as Independence Day and it is celebrated on the 4 July with fireworks, parades and festivities throughout the United States.

WASHINGTON, DC

USA North America

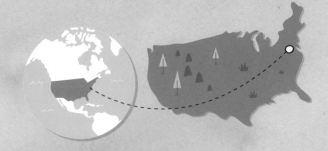

New York may be the USA's Big Apple, but Washington, DC is the country's capital. On the surface the city may appear stately and sombre – a place of grand ministerial buildings including the domed Capitol, the columned Treasury and the President's White House residence. Don't be fooled however, the streets also buzz with busy students, smart professionals and crowds of excited tourists.

MONEY, HOT OFF THE PRESS

Ker-ching! At the Bureau of Engraving and Printing you can watch real money being printed. If you had time to stand there all day you'd witness over $500 million roll off the presses. Before this new money goes into circulation, an equal amount of old money is removed. The average $1 bill lasts for 5.8 years before it gets too tattered for general use.

LUXEMBOURG

KENYA

MOROCCO

INDIA

ZAMBIA

THE TWO-TONE MONUMENT

The Washington Monument is the tallest structure in DC. It took so many years to build that the marble used to construct it had to come from different quarries. If you look closely, you can see the difference in colour where the old and new stone meet. The column honours the USA's first president and founding father George Washington. No building is allowed to be higher, by order of federal law.

CITY OF COUNTRIES

Washington, DC is home to more than 170 embassies from all around the world. If you step into one you are technically entering a foreign country, as the grounds are part of the embassy nation's territory. Visitors to DC can visit India, Kenya, Laos, Luxembourg, Malawi, Morocco and Zambia within an hour's walk!

WHITE HOUSE'S WEIRDEST RESIDENTS

Many presidents bring their pets with them when they move into the White House, but Theodore Roosevelt's family takes the prize. They arrived with a small bear, a lizard, five guinea pigs, a badger, a blue macaw, a hyena, a one-legged rooster, a barn owl, a pig, a rabbit, a hen and a pony, in addition to several dogs.

SQUEAK SQUEAK SQUEAK SQUEAK

G-R-R-R-R-R-!

COCK-A-DOODLE-DOO

NEIGH

WOOF WOOF WOOF WOOF

SMITHSONIAN TREASURES

Many people think the Smithsonian Institution is one place, but it's actually a group of 19 museums. The National Museum of American History shows Dorothy's ruby slippers from *The Wizard of Oz*, while the Air and Space National Museum displays the Wright Brothers' first plane. The National Museum of Natural History is home to the big, blue Hope Diamond. The gem is a beauty, but is said to bring tragedy to those who wear it. France's Marie Antoinette inherited the diamond in the 18th century, only to be beheaded by guillotine.

WORLD'S BIGGEST LIBRARY

The Library of Congress is the largest library in the world. A staggering 160 million books, photographs and maps are stored on 1,349km (838mi) of bookshelves. Imagine a bookcase that extends from Washington, DC to Chicago, and then another that stretches from Washington, DC to Philadelphia – the library's titles would barely fit on them! President Thomas Jefferson helped increase the library's collection when he offered 6,000 of his own books, several of which are still on display.

PHILADELPHIA

CHICAGO

WASHINGTON, DC

THE REAL ABRAHAM LINCOLN

More people visit the Lincoln Memorial than any other memorial in Washington, DC. Everyone wants to take a snap of the USA's most beloved president, and this statue is as good as it gets. Sculptors used 28 blocks of marble to make the likeness. Lincoln's face and hands are particularly realistic because they are based on castings made shortly before he died. Some people think that Abe looks sad, some think he looks thoughtful, and others believe that his expression changes depending on the angle you look from.

MIAMI

USA North America

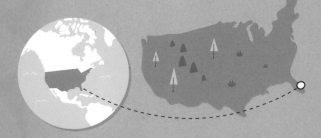

With colourful buildings, bags of sunshine and turquoise waves lapping on white sandy beaches, cities don't get much better than Miami! It's an outdoorsy place to be – made for speeding along the sidewalks on rollerblades or driving around town in a cool convertible. When the sun goes down, Miami comes alive as glamorous residents head to nightclubs and salsa dancing hotspots.

THE MOTHER OF MIAMI

Miami is the only major city in the USA to be founded by a woman. Julia Tuttle was the original owner of the land upon which the city was built. She persuaded rail chiefs to put in a train line to transport goods and people to the area. Soon a city was born, earning Julia the nickname 'Mother of Miami'.

TREASURE HUNT

Centuries ago, before the city was founded, gangs of pirates – including Blackbeard and his crew – ruled the bays around Miami. They would lurk in coves and inlets before setting sail to attack passing boats. Sometimes the loot would be buried for safekeeping, but if the pirate died, the location of his or her riches could be lost forever. Over the years many lucky treasure hunters have found gold, silver and gems in the waters around Miami.

THE WILD EVERGLADES

Miami is the gateway to the Everglades National Park. This vast wetland area provides a home to all kinds of wildlife, including rare animals such as manatees, sea turtles and Florida panthers. Visitors to the park can wander the boardwalks or whiz across the water in an airboat, keeping their eyes peeled for the Everglades' famous alligators.

THE MYSTERIES OF CORAL CASTLE

Coral Castle is an amazing tribute to the hard work and dedication of one man, Ed Leedskalnin. From 1923, Ed spent 28 years carving 997 tonnes (1,100 US tons) of rock into walls, sculptures, furniture, a tower and much more. It is mind-boggling to imagine one man making a castle using only basic tools, without any help to lift the heavy stones. Ed built Coral Castle in secret, but to this day no one knows how he did it.

CRUISE CAPITAL

Miami is the cruise ship capital of the world, with more passengers heading through its port than anywhere else. Most of the boats are bound for the nearby Caribbean, where holidaymakers can hop off their luxury ships and explore a different island each day.

MONKEYING AROUND

Ever wondered what it feels like to be an animal in a zoo? At Miami's Monkey Jungle you'll be the one in the cage while the animals are free to roam the 30-acre (12-hectare) forest around you. The park's large jungle spaces encourage a host of little squirrel monkeys, giant gorillas, noisy howler monkeys and chilled-out orangutans to live a similar life to their cousins in the wild.

LITTLE HAVANA

There is a corner of the city which feels like a different country entirely. The neighbourhood of Little Havana is home to a large number of Cubans and it looks much the same as their native country. The streets are full of colourful murals, Cuban restaurants, cigar shops, salsa dancing clubs and locals absorbed in games of dominoes – Cuba's favourite pastime.

HAVANA

CUBA North America

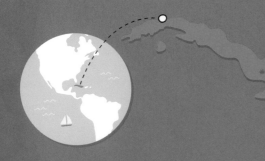

Cuba is unlike anywhere else on Earth. In the capital, Havana, visitors feel like they've taken a time machine back to the 1950s. Vintage cars chug along streets lined with beautiful, crumbling old buildings, while simple pleasures like salsa dancing and dominoes are the favourite ways to have fun.

COMMUNIST CUBA

Cuba is a communist country, which means that life here is very different to most other places in the world. Communists believe that everyone should be equal and have the same amount. In Havana, wages are low and until 2011 people were not allowed to own their own homes – if they wanted to move they had to swap properties. After 50 years, the country is starting to relax some of its strictest rules however, so life in the city could soon change.

HEALTHY HAVANA

Feeling sick? Havana may be one of the best places in the world to be poorly. There are more doctors per person here than anywhere else on the planet! People in Cuba also live longer than in many other North and South American countries.

CHEAP EATS

In Havana everyone has a ration book, enabling them to buy foods and groceries at a very cheap price. Essentials like rice, beans and sugar are bought from the nearby *bodega* (local store). As the average Cuban salary works out at only US$20 per month, people don't have much money to spend on eating out. Luckily in Havana the streets are filled with food vendors selling cheap and tasty treats from stands, wheelbarrows, baskets and windows.

CLASSIC CARS

Havana's streets are like a living classic car museum. Vintage rides are the norm because for five decades only an elite group of people were allowed to buy new vehicles. This meant that everyone else was stuck with cars from the 1950s! The law has recently changed and people are now allowed to purchase new vehicles if they want to. The cars cost so much however, very few can actually afford them.

DANCING THE NIGHT AWAY

Two of the world's most famous dances began in Havana. Sultry salsa and lively mambo both started life in the city's streets before spreading their infectious rhythms to the rest of the globe.

FIDEL CASTRO

In July 1959, Fidel Castro became the leader of Cuba and turned it into a communist nation. He ruled for nearly 50 years before passing the reins of power to his brother, Raúl Castro. Fidel is known for banning everything American from Cuba. This means that you won't find McDonalds, Coca Cola or other big US brands in Havana.

KINGSTON
JAMAICA North America

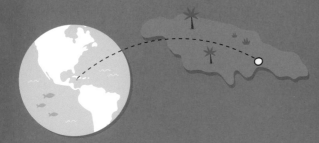

Kingston may be a small city on a small island, but it has made a big impact on the world. The city is famous for its cool, laidback style and toe-tapping reggae music, as well as being home to some of the fastest athletes on the planet. Jamaica's colourful capital is squeezed between the Blue Mountains and a deep, natural harbour.

RASTAFARI
Rastafari is a religion that developed in Kingston in the 1930s. Followers often have dreadlocks (matted coils of hair) just like the faith's most famous believer, Bob Marley. Although Rastafari isn't Jamaica's main religion, its colours of red, green and gold can be seen throughout the city, with many people linking it to Bob and reggae music.

SAFE HARBOUR
Kingston Harbour stretches almost 16km (10mi) wide, making it one of the biggest natural harbours in the world. With just a narrow entrance guarded by two forts, the harbour was well protected from invaders back when the waters of the Caribbean were lawless. The bodies of dead pirates were sometimes hung at the entrance to give unwanted visitors an idea of what could happen if they attempted to raid the harbour.

EMANCIPATION PARK
Jamaica was ruled by the British for more than 300 years. During this time, huge numbers of slaves from West Africa were brought to the island to work on sugarcane farms. In 1838 freedom (also called 'emancipation') was finally given to the slaves, allowing them to choose what they wanted to do with their lives. Kingston's Emancipation Park is not just a pretty escape from the hustle and bustle of the city — it's an important symbol of Jamaican freedom.

THE PIRATE CITY OF PORT ROYAL
Hundreds of years ago, the city of Port Royal at the edge of Kingston Harbour was a base for many pirates of the Caribbean. The rum-drinking scoundrels were known for their bad behaviour, leading people to describe the place as the 'wickedest city on Earth'. In 1692 however, Port Royal was hit by an earthquake so powerful, two thirds of the land and buildings were sent tumbling into the sea. It never bounced back, leading neighbouring Kingston to grow and become the harbour's biggest city instead.

NICE AND SPICY

'Jerk' may be an insult in some parts of the world, but in Kingston it is a much-loved savoury dish with a hot and fiery flavour. Jerk is made by coating meat – usually chicken, pork or goat – in a tasty sauce or blend of dry spices before barbecuing. Delicious!

WINTER OLYMPICS

In the 1988 Winter Olympics, Kingston surprised the world by entering the bobsleigh event. As the athletes came from a tropical island, they were not used to cold temperatures and had had limited practice with bobsleighs. Not surprisingly Jamaica didn't fare well. They finished in 30th place in the two-man race and crashed in the four-man event, leading the team to famously push their sled along the rest of the course. The crowd loved them anyway, and in their first ever Winter Olympics Jamaica was the most talked about team at the Games.

REGGAE FEVER

Reggae music was born in Jamaica then made famous across the globe by the legendary Kingston musician, Bob Marley. The singer and songwriter became known for his catchy tunes about love, freedom and changing the world.

WAH GWAN

TALKING THE TALK

In Kingston, people speak English with a unique twist. Over the centuries the island has blended English, African and other languages together to create its own singsong dialect. Some of the words and phrases – such as ''wah gwan?'', which means ''what's going on?'' – are spoken not just in Kingston, but by Jamaican communities all around the world.

MEXICO CITY
MEXICO North America

Mexico City is full of surprises. It is a place where you can buy voodoo dolls at the market, eat insects for dinner and wander through streets lined with buildings that are disappearing into the ground. It is also famously busy, with 20 million inhabitants all eating, sleeping and working side by side.

A SMOGGY SOLUTION

Mexico City is one of the most polluted places in the world, but it is finding some unique ways to clean up its act. One hospital even eats the smog created by cars. The hospital's walls react with the smog and break it down so that the fumes are no longer harmful, helping to improve the air for dwellers across the city.

CHOMPING ON CREEPY CRAWLIES

Mexico City has some amazing street food, with stalls serving up *tacos*, *burritos* and everything in between. Insects have also become a popular choice. Many fancy restaurants in the city have ant larvae, stink bugs and other creepy crawlies on their menus! As the demand for bugs has shot up, so have the prices. Farmers can make a lot of money from selling giant winged ants and other exotic insects.

MUSEUM MANIA

Mexico City claims to have more museums than any other city on the planet. With so many to choose from there is something for every interest, from an antique toy museum to a shoe museum or even a museum just for pens. One of the city's most striking buildings is the Soumaya Museum. The modern art space is clad in more than 16,000 hexagonal, metal plates. The plates don't touch the ground or one another, making it look as if they are floating.

MAGICAL MARKET

When people want to mend a broken heart, wreak revenge on an enemy or treat a health complaint, one of the places they turn to is Sonora Market. Devoted to witchcraft and the occult, the market is packed with magical wares – browsers will find spiritual cleansing, voodoo dolls, remedies and potions all for sale on its tabletops.

THAT SINKING FEELING

Mexico City is sinking at an alarming rate. Around the city, buildings are tilting and edging into the earth as the ground begins to swallow them whole. The problem is down to the lack of water underneath the city. Vast quantities are pumped up to be used above the surface, leaving a void that makes the ground sink. As the population grows, more water is needed and the city's buildings get lower and lower.

LUCHA LIBRE

Watching masked wrestlers take to the ring and unleash high-flying acrobatic moves on their opponents is a favourite pastime for locals in Mexico City. *Lucha libre* is the most popular sport in the country after soccer – thousands turn out to cheer on their favourite competitors every week. The wrestlers are famous for their exciting, daredevil moves and colourful costumes. The best in the ring quickly become household names.

ISLAND OF THE DOLLS

The Island of the Dolls is one of Mexico City's strangest sights. On a small island in the canals south of the city, hundreds of dolls and their broken-off heads and limbs hang eerily from the trees. This creepy looking display is in memory of a young girl who drowned nearby.

OAXACA CITY

MEXICO North America

The city of Oaxaca (pronounced 'waa-hah-kah') in southern Mexico is rich in history and traditions. It also is one of the most popular spots for celebrating the Day of the Dead festival. The annual event is an important holiday in the Mexican calendar – a time when the whole city comes together to honour the departed.

CANDLELIT CEMETERIES

Oaxaca's cemeteries are the centre of the Day of the Dead celebrations. Families gather around the tombs of deceased loved ones, holding vigils throughout the night. The cemeteries are incredible sights, with candles and flowers surrounding the graves, along with crowds of picnicking families, musicians and costumed revellers.

FESTIVAL FOOD

Oaxaca is famous for its lip-smackingly good food such as *tamales* (corn dough with various fillings wrapped in banana leaf) and roasted grasshoppers. During the Day of the Dead, families eat the favourite dishes of their deceased relatives along with some special foods such as 'bread of the dead' (sweet rolls decorated with bone shapes). *Champurrado* is a thick, hot, chocolatey drink often served with *churros* (crispy fingers of fried dough). Sweet-toothed locals can't get enough of the stuff!

RETURN OF THE DEAD

The holiday is celebrated on 1-2 November – this is when Mexicans believe the dead are able to make a brief return to visit the living. To help the deceased find their way, arches of yellow flowers are created as gateways to the spirit world. Families also build altars stacked with offerings such as flowers, candles and foods, along with water in case the spirits get thirsty. The first day of the festival is dedicated to dead children and so favourite toys are also given up to the spirit world.

DEAD HAPPY

Thinking of loved ones who have died sounds sad and sombre, but the Day of the Dead is the opposite of this. It is a joyful celebration with music, parades, costumes, feasts and funfairs. Skeletons can be found everywhere you look in Oaxaca City at this time – as plastic toys, sculptures, pictures and costumes – but they are not supposed to be scary. The skeletons are usually shown looking cheerful and doing everyday activities such as riding a bike or playing musical instruments.

LA PAZ

BOLIVIA South America

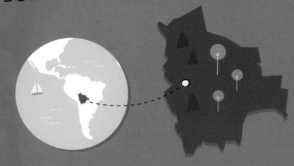

Take a deep breath – the air is thin in the high-altitude city of La Paz. Bolivia's capital sits in a bowl-shaped valley, surrounded by the peaks of the Andes mountains. This part of the South American *Altiplano*, or 'high plateau', is the long-time home of the Inca and Aymara peoples. Today modern skyscrapers rise up from the canyon and urban cable cars sway overhead.

THE HIGHEST CAPITAL IN THE WORLD

At an altitude of 3,660m (12,007ft) above sea level, La Paz is the highest capital city on Earth. The locals go about their everyday lives at the same elevation as the world's loftiest ski resorts! Buildings cling precariously to the steep slopes around the edge of the canyon, spilling down towards the centre of town. La Paz often has its head in the clouds, but residents have to be wary of other weather conditions, too. Sun, rain and snow can be much harsher than they are down at sea level.

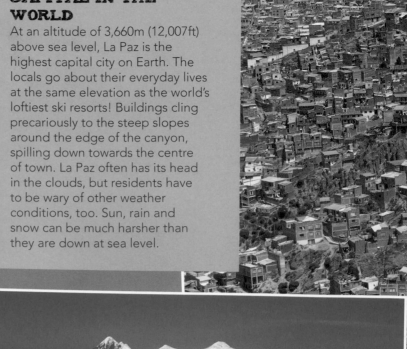

SNOWY PEAKS

Even on a warm, sunny day in La Paz, snow glitters in the distance. The city is set against a dramatic mountain range called the Cordillera Real. The tallest of its peaks, the Illimani, is snow-capped all year round. The highest tip of the Illimani's four summits clocks in at a soaring 6,438m (21,122ft)! As well as being famously difficult to climb, the mountain has become an iconic symbol for both La Paz and the Bolivian nation. As the local song goes, *'Illimani, Illimani, patrimonio eres de Bolivia'* – 'Illimani, Illimani, you are Bolivia's heritage'!

HIGH-ALTITUDE HEADACHE

Feeling dizzy or drowsy? Finding it hard to catch your breath? It can take a little while to adjust to the thin air in La Paz. Many people need to spend a few days taking it easy before their lungs adjust to the city's high elevation. Locals call altitude sickness *soroche* and they have a special remedy for it – the coca plant. Its green leaf is brewed like a hot tea infusion.

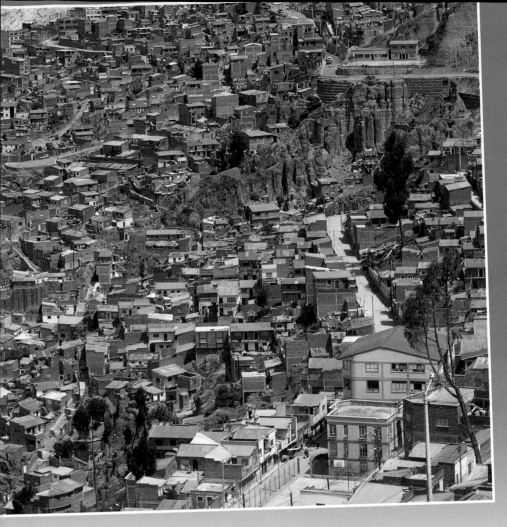

A NEVERENDING RUNWAY

Aeroplanes come into La Paz via El Alto airport, the highest international airport in the world. Up at this altitude, the low pressure creates reduced air resistance, making the planes move incredibly fast. They need special tyres to handle the high speeds and extra-long runways to land on. When an aircraft has touched down it has to taxi for longer in order to bring down its speed and finally reach a stop.

A RIDE IN THE SKY

La Paz is very crowded, so traffic congestion can prove a problem. When the streets get too full, many skip the bus and go for a ride in the sky instead. La Paz has the largest urban cable-car system in the world, with three lines in operation, and plans for six more in the works. Many travellers commute between La Paz and the neighbouring city of El Alto this way. When the proposed system is complete, the sky-high cars will carry as many as 27,000 passengers in a single hour!

DEATH ROAD

The Camino a Los Yungas, nicknamed the 'Death Road', plummets from the heights of La Paz to the depths of the Amazon rainforest. The two-lane road measures a mere 3.2m (10.5ft) across, lined with solid rock on one side and the edge of a high cliff on the other. Hundreds of people die on the hairpin turns of the Death Road every year, but intrepid cyclists and adventurers are constantly turning up to test their luck. As well as tight bends and plunging ravines, the road often succumbs to mudslides, falling rocks and thick, rolling fog.

CARTAGENA
COLOMBIA South America

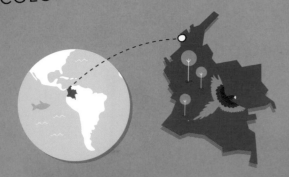

Cartagena de Indias is a charming port with a stormy past – in the 16th and 17th centuries, the settlement was a magnet for pillaging pirates! So many plunderers set their sights on Cartagena and its gold, a wall had to be built around the city. Nowadays visitors are free to explore the old fortifications and ride boats in the bay where pirate ships once used to roam.

PIRATES OF THE CARIBBEAN
An approaching ship waving the Jolly Roger flag was a sign to turn round and flee – the black skull and crossbones meant that pirates were coming your way! Most of the buccaneers that came into Cartagena threatening lives and demanding gold were French and English. One French pirate named Baal invaded the city while the governor was dining at a banquet. After a dramatic swordfight, Baal pocketed a handsome ransom in gold then escaped before the stunned guests could stop him.

ALL THAT GLITTERS
The ancient craft of the Zenú tribe is astonishing to behold. The tribe created incredibly intricate gilded objects including jaguar sculptures, jewel-laden hammocks and trees decorated with tiny gleaming bells. The gold that has caused so much drama in Cartagena's history is now on display at the city's *Museo de Oro* (Museum of Gold). The display cases shine with sacred relics, gravediggers' spoils and pirates' booty.

TREASURE TROVE
The city of Cartagena was founded by Spanish explorers in 1533. The Spanish seized the fabulous riches of the region's native peoples, including the Inca, then established the city as an important stop on the European trade route. Ships carrying gold, silver and silk from Peru and Ecuador used to dock in Cartagena before sailing back to Spain. All of this newfound wealth soon caught the attention of pirate crews, however. The city was sieged five times in the 16th century alone!

LIFE'S A BREEZE

Cartagena's locals are used to hustle and bustle – the city is crowded, hot and sticky. Street vendors jostle at every turn, and when they're not in school their children often come and help out. On Sundays however, many families like to escape the heat and fly kites together outside the city walls. A colourful festival takes place every August, when the winds are especially strong.

THE IMPENETRABLE FORT

The Castillo de San Felipe de Barajas is the only stronghold in Cartagena that pirates never managed to invade and conquer. It's the largest Spanish colonial fortress outside of Spain – protected by thick walls, formidable bunkers and powerful parapets. An eerie maze of tunnels connects key locations deep inside the fort. The tunnels were carefully designed so that even the slightest noise echoes through the gloomy corridors, making it impossible for an enemy to approach without being detected.

SELF-DEFENCE

Once the Spanish had a stockpile of treasure, they needed to find a way to protect it. The government decided to build a wall around the Colombian city, as well as several other walled compounds and castles. The plan wasn't entirely successful, but by the start of the 17th century Cartagena was considered the best-protected city in South America.

ONE WAY IN, ONE WAY OUT

In the 17th century, there was only one way into Cartagena's walled city – everybody had to file through the old Clock Tower Gate. There was only one central door, making it easy to keep unwanted visitors out! Although three doors are open now, the gateway is still the most famous landmark in Cartagena. It used to have a weapons room and a chapel inside, but today the tower features a huge Swiss clock instead.

GRAVE-DIGGING FOR GOLD

Cartagena's treasure came from deep underground. The Zenú tribe lived in the region from 200 BC to around 1600, and gold was a central part of their culture. When a great Zenú leader died, they were buried with all of their most precious possessions. Spanish explorers discovered these tombs full of gleaming gold and started looting the burial sites, amassing a great pile of riches.

MANAUS
BRAZIL South America

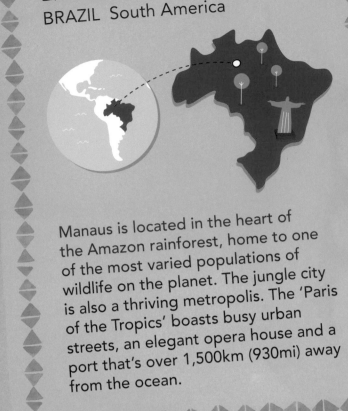

Manaus is located in the heart of the Amazon rainforest, home to one of the most varied populations of wildlife on the planet. The jungle city is also a thriving metropolis. The 'Paris of the Tropics' boasts busy urban streets, an elegant opera house and a port that's over 1,500km (930mi) away from the ocean.

THE JUNGLE CITY

Manaus doesn't have as many parks as other cities because it is surrounded by green space! Manaus is so close to the Amazon rainforest, the boundary between the two worlds – the urban realm of humans, and the natural kingdom of wild animals – isn't always clear. It's not uncommon to see brilliantly feathered birds flying over rooftops or to spot a reptile scuttling down a side street. When humans venture into the rainforest however, they are more wary. Most take organized tours or travel with a guide who knows how to stay safe out in the jungle!

COMMUTING BY CANOE

Where Venice has canals, Manaus has *igarapés*. In the local Nheengatu language, the word means 'canoe path', referring to the complex system of streams, tributaries and small rivers that knot and weave through the city.

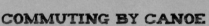

SLEEPING IN THE TREETOPS

Manaus is home to the largest treetop hotel in the world, the Ariau Amazon Towers. The design was inspired by the oceanographer, Jacques Cousteau. Cousteau is said to have come up with the idea of creating a huge building on stilts using traditional rainforest materials. The hotel rooms are set high in the forest canopy, connected to each other by over 8km (5mi) of wooden walkways.

WATERY MEETING

There's an unusual sight in Manaus called the Encontro das Águas, or the 'Meeting of Waters'. It's the place where two rivers collide – the dark Rio Negro and the lighter, sandy-coloured Amazon. The rivers have different temperatures and densities, and they also move at different speeds. Instead of mixing, the two bodies of water flow next to each other for several kilometres. Fascinated travellers make boat trips to watch the dark and light currents running side by side.

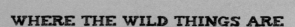

WHERE THE WILD THINGS ARE

Pink dolphins, scarlet macaws, red howler monkeys, piranhas, alligators and spiders – the rainforest around Manaus is crawling with creatures. Scientists have counted up more than 1,300 types of birds, at least 400 mammal varieties, another 400 amphibians, around 375 kinds of reptiles and a staggering 40,000 different types of plants. There is one species you won't find many of, however. On average, there is less than one human being for every square kilometre (0.4 square mile) of land. Imagine a space 11 football fields long and 11 fields wide – that's a whole lot of room for a single person!

A NIGHT AT THE OPERA

A fancy theatre in the middle of the jungle isn't the first thing you might expect to see, but the Amazonas Opera House is one of the grandest in South America. The building was constructed when Brazil was at its richest, after a boom in selling rubber. Imported French glass and glossy Italian marble stand as proof that no expense was spared. The black and white tilework near the entrance was inspired by something much more local, however – the meeting of the dark and light Rio Negro and Amazon rivers.

RIDING THE TIDES

You might have heard of buildings that are constructed to withstand earthquakes, but what about a structure that's built to rise and fall with the tides? Manaus' Porto Flutuante is a floating dock lined with restaurants and shops. If the tide is coming in while you're ordering lunch, you could be sitting up much higher by the time the bill arrives!

RIO DE JANEIRO
BRAZIL South America

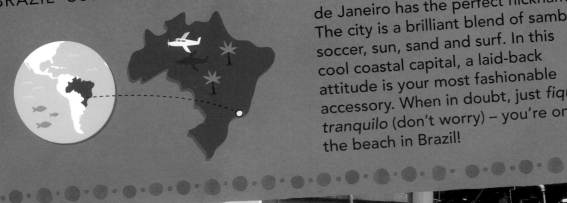

Life's a beach in the *Cidade Maravilhosa* (Marvellous City)! Rio de Janeiro has the perfect nickname. The city is a brilliant blend of samba, soccer, sun, sand and surf. In this cool coastal capital, a laid-back attitude is your most fashionable accessory. When in doubt, just *fique tranquilo* (don't worry) – you're on the beach in Brazil!

FLAMBOYANT FAVELAS

The colourful houses on the hillsides of Rio are independent communities called *favelas* – small cities within a larger city. *Favelas* emerged in Rio after slavery was abolished. Former slaves, poor men and women with few opportunities to work, gathered together in crowded and basic settlements. Some *favelas* are still extremely poor, while others are flourishing hotbeds of creative activity. These streets and houses inspire resident artists and travellers alike with their vibrant colours and culture.

SUGARLOAF

Pão de Açúcar (Sugarloaf) is a mountain with a funny name and a very funny shape. It is one of Rio's most famous natural landmarks, rising 396m (1,299ft) above Guanabara Bay. Before sugar cubes were invented, sugar was sold in sugarloaves. The mounds of refined sugar were formed into tall cones with rounded tops, just like the shape of the famous mountain.

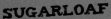

CHRIST THE REDEEMER

Standing high on the peak of Corcovado mountain, the iconic Christ the Redeemer is a powerful symbol of Rio de Janeiro. It's the largest Art Deco sculpture in the world, created in a style that favours simplified, flowing shapes. The mighty statue, designed by French sculptor Paul Landowski, is a perfect example of Art Deco design. Made of concrete and soapstone, the statue is a towering 30m (98ft) tall, with arms that stretch 28m (92ft) wide. It was completed in 1931.

LIFE BY THE SEA

Copacabana is one of the most famous beaches in the world. Skateboarders and in-line skaters on the beachfront sail past sunbathers in teeny-tiny swimsuits, teams square off in *futebol* (football) and beach volleyball matches, surfers take to the crashing waves and vendors sell everything from coconuts to beach blankets. Young people practise *capoeira* on the sand – a unique hybrid of dance and self-defence invented and developed by African slaves during the 16th century.

GIRL FROM IPANEMA

The second most recorded pop song in history, just behind the Beatles' *Yesterday*, is *Garota de Ipanema (The Girl From Ipanema)*. The classic tune was written in 1962, and inspired by a real-life Rio resident. Nineteen-year-old Heloísa Eneida Menezes Paes Pinto lived in the fashionable oceanfront neighbourhood called Ipanema. On her way to the beach every day she walked past the Veloso café, where the song's composers often sat. Translated from Portuguese, the lyrics to the song go, "Tall and tan and young and lovely, the girl from Ipanema goes walking… when she walks she's like a samba, that swings so cool and sways so gentle…".

CRAZY FOR COCONUTS

The beverage of choice in Rio is *água de coco* (coconut water). Up and down the city's beaches and streets, machete-wielding vendors slice the tops off chilled green coconuts, then pop straws into the openings.

THE BEAUTIFUL GAME

Brazilian *futebol* superstar Pelé called his sport *o jogo bonito*, meaning 'the beautiful game'. Football is an integral part of Brazilian culture and lifestyle, popular with all ages. It is played everywhere from beaches to city plazas to patches of grass on the side of the highway. The most famous venue in Rio de Janeiro is the Maracanã stadium, opened for the World Cup in 1950. Today the stadium hosts matches between Rio's rival teams.

RIO DE JANEIRO

Each year, Rio explodes into a huge open-air party and everyone is invited! According to the Christian calendar, Carnival is a traditional celebration that takes place in February or March during the lead-up to Lent. Rio's version is the largest celebration in the world, attracting two million revellers to the city streets every day.

STIFF COMPETITION

At the very heart of Carnival is an intense competition between Rio's top samba schools. Fifteen perform at the Sambadrome in the first two days of the Carnival festivities, but the top twelve vie for the championship at the end of the celebrations. Each samba school's parade tells a story. The crowds are guaranteed outrageous costumes, original music, creative choreography and a few special surprises!

DRESS CODE

Fabulous feathers, shiny sequins, glitter, towering headdresses, over-the-top platform shoes – the samba schools' costumes are out of this world. Just one costumed samba dancer makes an incredible sight. Picture what it's like to see hundreds of them parading before your eyes all at once!

KNOW THE LINGO

Blocos and bandas are percussion bands that parade through the streets, playing traditional samba music. Hundreds of groups participate in Rio's Carnival every year, and each has its own culture, style and set of traditions, including a signature song. People of all ages and walks of life take to the streets, and anyone can join the march. Many wear a costume or buy their favourite bloco's official shirt.

POWER COUPLE

The Porta Bandeira, or 'Flag Bearer', is at the head of every samba school's parade. She is the most important woman in the show. Her duties include performing difficult samba steps, charming the crowd and the judges, and carrying the flag without letting it touch her body. Just a brush is an infraction that could cost her school a few precious points! At her side is the Mestre Sala (Ballroom Master), a male protector and guide who leads the Porta Bandeira on her way through the Sambadrome.

THE SAMBADROME
The five days of *Carnaval* (Carnival) include a national two-day holiday filled with dancing and music, fabulous floats and colourful costumes. Parties and parades take place all over town, but the centre of the action is the Sambadrome Marquês de Sapucaí, a huge exhibition space designed by the Brazilian architect, Oscar Niemeyer. The Sambadrome is lined on either side with grandstands so that spectators can watch the action below. It is also the location of Carnival's spectacular opening ceremonies. The space is freshly painted white each year, allowing the vibrant colours of the performers' costumes to really pop!

FANCIFUL FLOATS
After the *Porta Bandeira* come the floats. Like the dancers' costumes, each one is outrageous and elaborate. Each float is unique and highly detailed, featuring several levels of sculptures and decorations, plus platforms for the dancers to stand on as they entertain the crowds below.

CUZCO
PERU South America

Cuzco is one of the oldest continually inhabited cities in the Western Hemisphere. Once the capital of the great Inca empire, it was later colonized by Spanish explorers. The rich heritage of these two fused cultures remains in Cuzco today. Bowler hat wearing locals lead llamas up the cobblestone streets, while fine boutiques and hotels cater for the tourists heading on to the ruins of Machu Picchu.

GOLDEN TEMPLE

Only the stone foundations remain today, but Qorikancha (meaning 'Golden Courtyard' in the local language of Quechua) was once the richest temple in the entire Inca empire. Built around the year 1200, the temple was full of solid-gold artefacts, including sculptures of llamas and babies, and life-sized replicas of corn used in rituals. Even the building itself was gilded – the walls were lined with at least 700 heavy gold sheets!

STONE SURPRISE

Nobody knows exactly how the beautiful city of Cuzco was built. Where did all the rocks come from? How were they transported? How did the builders cut them so precisely? It's said that 16th century Spanish settlers were stunned at the incredible stonework they discovered here. The carvings are far more intricate and sturdy than anything seen in Europe at that time.

SACRED PUMA

The centre of Cuzco was carefully designed in the shape of a puma, a sacred animal in ancient Inca culture. The puma's head was the fortress of Sacsahuaman, the rivers Tulumayo and Huatanay outlined the shape of its body, and the tail was formed by Pumaq Chupan, the place where the two rivers come together. The puma's heart was the holy central square, home to Qorikancha temple.

MACHU PICCHU

Cuzco is the gateway to Machu Picchu, the world-famous ruins of the ancient Inca. Although it's only 80km (50mi) away from the city, getting there can be tricky! Visitors can arrive by helicopter, trundle up hair-raising hairpin bends in a bus or mini-van, or hike the steep Inca trail. Many, however, plump for the three-hour train ride. Tourists choose between traditional engines with luxurious wood-panelled restaurant cars and modern trains with glass-domed roofs. Machu Picchu is tucked between two towering peaks of the Andes. The 'city in the clouds' offers a mysterious and marvellous glimpse into an advanced and lost society. It is one of the New Seven Wonders of the World.

EARTHQUAKE

Cuzco is often hit by earthquakes, caused by friction between massive chunks of the Earth's crust. While the shaking ground often topples modern structures, it is astonishing that ancient Inca buildings remain standing. The Incas didn't use mortar to secure their walls, but instead cut individual stones out exactly and wedged them together. During an earthquake, it's said that the stones in an Inca wall 'dance' – moving together gently before settling back into place when the shaking stops.

GUINEA PIGGING OUT!

Feeling peckish? *Cuy* (guinea pig) is a traditional delicacy in Peru and a menu staple at restaurants and food markets all around Cuzco. The plump rodent is usually fried or roasted whole, served with a crispy coat of garlic and salt and then eaten with the hands.

BUENOS AIRES
ARGENTINA South America

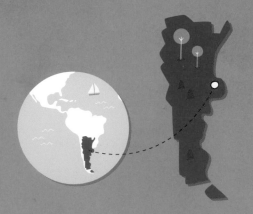

THE CANDY BOX
One of the city's famous landmarks – the home stadium for Boca Juniors, one of Buenos Aires' leading *fútbol* teams – is nicknamed *La Bombonera* (the Candy Box) due to its unusual shape. When Boca plays their rival, River Plate, the stadium fills to its capacity of 49,000 and the whole place seems to shake as excited fans in the stands jump up and down.

Buenos Aires moves to the rhythm of the tango. The birthplace of this dramatic dance is a city famous for its passion – for friends and family, music, the fine arts and of course, *fútbol* (football).

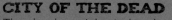

CITY OF THE DEAD
The dead aren't buried underground in Buenos Aires – at least not the most influential people. Occupying over 5 hectares (14 acres) in the middle of one of the city's wealthiest neighbourhoods, the Recoleta Cemetery is made up of more than 4,000 above ground tombs and vaults. The elegant marble mausoleums are laid out in rows, like streets. They hold the remains of Argentinian presidents, Nobel Prize winners, and Eva Perón, better known as 'Evita'.

THE GIANT RUBBER TREE
Go ahead, hug a tree! If you want to do it in Buenos Aires however, you'll need to bring some friends. The city is filled with giant rubber trees with twisting roots that look like the tentacles of an octopus. The most famous tree, nicknamed the Gran Gomero, is in Plaza Francia. It was planted in 1791 and measures an impressive 50m (164ft) wide!

A BOOKSTORE IN A THEATRE

It's not every day that you can browse biographies in the orchestra pit, look at art books on the mezzanine, and enjoy hot chocolate on the stage. You can at El Ateneo Grand Splendid, a glamorous old theatre that's been converted into a bookstore, complete with a café and restaurant on the stage where tango legend Carlos Gardel once performed.

DULCE DE LECHE

What's that irresistible caramel spread? It's dulce de leche! It is found in every café, ice cream parlour and bakery. Children enjoy it with toast or pastries as part of their afternoon merienda (snack).

WALLS THAT TALK

A boy who's three storeys tall, a walrus the size of a small apartment building, a turtle as big as a garage door? You'll find these characters and many, many more rendered in colourful paint all over walls in Buenos Aires. That's because, unlike in many other major cities, there are no laws prohibiting artists from using outdoor surfaces as giant canvases. The walls of Buenos Aires have tales to tell.

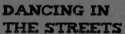

DANCING IN THE STREETS

Tango was born in Buenos Aires. By the time the dance form became popular in Paris in 1912, it was the symbol of glamour. But in its birthplace, tango had humble origins – it was practised in the side streets and bars of immigrant communities around the port. Today, Argentinians love to show off the dance, performing in public spaces to the accompaniment of traditional tango music.

THE WIDEST AVENUE

It takes a long time to cross Avenida 9 de Julio. The avenue – named after 9 July, Argentina's Independence Day – is the widest of any city in the world. Some days it stretches 12 lanes wide, other times there are as many as 16. The avenue runs through the centre of the city, linking up two important train stations – Retiro and Constitución. It's said that the quickest you can cross it on foot, if you pay attention to the signs and walk quickly, is around two and a half minutes.

USHUAIA

ARGENTINA South America

Remote and snow-covered, Ushuaia is the capital of Tierra del Fuego – an island known as the 'land of fire'. It's the southernmost city in the world, just a boat ride away from icy Antarctica. Despite Ushuaia's faraway feel, the city is expanding fast. Streets dot the slopes as the Andes Mountains sweep down to meet the southern shores.

ANCIENT NOMADS

Ushuaia was untouched by Europeans for most of its history. For thousands of years, the land was the home of two peoples, the Selk'nam and the Yaghan. Both nomadic tribes were hunter-gatherers who walked around almost naked despite the cold climate. To stay warm, they rubbed their bodies with seal grease and stayed close to the fire at night.

THE END OF THE WORLD

Ushuaia sits in a bay on Tierra del Fuego, in between the Martial Mountain range and the Beagle Channel, a strait that separates the large main island from lots of smaller ones. The eastern part of the strait also forms the border between Chile and Argentina. The channel was named after the *HMS Beagle*, the first English ship that navigated the waters.

PENGUIN ISLAND

Penguins rule and the humans are outsiders on Isla Martillo, a tiny island in the Beagle Channel. Around 3,000 pairs of Gentoo and Magellanic penguins live in the colony. In order to protect this natural habitat and its roly-poly black and white residents, human access is carefully restricted. Only a limited number of people are allowed to walk on the island each day, under the watch of a licensed guide. Penguins swim, play and waddle across the paths, while their fuzzy chicks huddle together in the breeze.

A COLOSSAL CRAB

The *centolla* (king crab) might look too dangerous to eat, but it is a speciality in Ushuaia! At some restaurants, the staff allow guests to pick out their own crab for dinner. After it's weighed and steamed, the waiter brings the *centolla* to the table with tools to help break through the shell and sample the juicy, delicious meat inside. It can be a messy business, so everyone wears a bib to protect their clothes.

WILD WEATHER

Ushuaia has a subpolar climate, which means that the weather is cold all year-round. Even in the warmest summer months the average temperature is only 10°C (50°F). The weather is also famously unpredictable. It's not uncommon for a storm to sweep in on a sunny afternoon, warning all of the boat captains to return to the port. It snows regularly in Ushuaia too, particularly in the winter months of July and August, when crowds go skiing and snowboarding in the mountains outside of town. Most locals work in industries like fishing, sheep farming, natural gas and oil extraction, plus of course, tourism. Lots of people want to come and visit the end of the world!

A LONELY LIGHTHOUSE

An iconic red and white landmark stands guard at the sea entrance to Ushuaia – the Les Eclaireurs lighthouse. The lighthouse has been in service for nearly a century, but these days it's uninhabited and operated by a remote control! The beacon flashes every ten seconds, and the light can be seen 7.5 nautical miles (14km/8.6mi) away.

A WALL OF ICE

You've seen pictures of glaciers on bottles of mineral water, but have you ever had an ice-cold drink directly from a glacier? El Martial glacier towers high above the bay in Ushuaia, providing the city's main source of fresh water. A chairlift travels up the wall of ice, offering amazing views of the Beagle Channel below.

61

REYKJAVÍK
ICELAND Europe

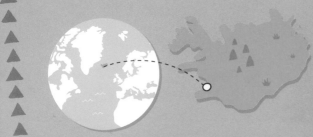

Life in the planet's most northerly capital is never boring. Reykjavík sits pretty on the western shores of the land of ice and fire – Iceland. The city is surrounded by volatile volcanoes on one side and a bay full of Arctic animals on the other. People bathe in hot springs, make amazing art and explore the great outdoors, just like their Viking ancestors before them.

PONGY WATER!
The city's hot water comes from a different source to the cold and is full of eggy-smelling sulphur. It's really stinky and shouldn't be drunk. The cold water, however, is completely safe to drink – in fact it's some of the purest H_2O on the planet. The extra sulphur in the warm shower water does have some uses, however. After a few baths it will make your skin feel baby soft.

NOISY NEIGHBOURS
The volcanic Bláfjöll (Blue Mountains) are visible from Reykjavík, and people from the city often go skiing there. The most recent eruption was in 1389, but volcanic activity in this area goes in cycles of 800 to 1,000 years. Things could get interesting anytime soon…

HUFFIN' AND PUFFIN
Reykjavík is located on Faxaflói Bay, which is also home to thousands of puffins and marine mammals, including minke whales, humpbacks and orcas. Whale watching trips from the city's old harbour are massively popular, but the mammals are still hunted and eaten here, too. Some local restaurants even sell whale and puffin burgers.

HOT PROPERTY
Popular Reykjavík souvenirs include ancient rocks, pumice stones, bottles of ash and jewellery made from lava that spews from the volcanoes surrounding the city.

STEAM POWERED

Reykjavík means 'Smoke Cove' – named after the steam rising from cracks in the Earth's crust, which are found all around the city. Even in Iceland's winter, people forget their frozen surroundings and tiptoe through the snow to go swimming in giant outdoor pools such as Laugardalslaug and the Blue Lagoon on the Reykjanes Peninsula. The water is thermally heated by energy under the Earth's surface.

CHOSEN BY GODS

Reykjavík was founded by a Viking chief called Ingólfur Arnarson, whose name means 'royal wolf'. He rocked up on Iceland's uninhabited coast in 874, fleeing a feud in his native Norway. Arnarson chose his new home the traditional way – by throwing some symbolic wooden poles into the ocean and allowing the gods to decide where they washed ashore. According to the ancient *Íslendingabók (Book of Iceland)*, it took his slaves Vífill and Karli three years to find the jettisoned poles.

LIKE A VIKING?

In Reykjavík you can go back in time and explore a 10th century Viking longhouse that was lost for a thousand years until being rediscovered in 2001. There's also a bloodthirsty theatre and exhibition centre called the Saga Museum that teaches people about Iceland's violent Viking past.

ELF HELP

Many Icelanders believe in elves, dwarves and other mystical mythical beings, traditionally known as *huldufolk* (hidden people). Next door to Reykjavík is Hafnarfjörður, famous for having Iceland's largest population of elves. There's an elf park, and expert tour guides can point out the little people's dwellings.

People recently protested against a road being built through a lava field into Reykjavík because it would upset the local elves.

TROMSØ

NORWAY Europe

Tromsø is known as the 'Land of the Midnight Sun'. The city lies so far north that for two months every summer, there is daylight 24/7. In the depths of winter however, the polar night lasts all day. Children go to school in the dark, with only the Moon and its reflection in the snow casting natural light.

LONGEST DAY
People often have trouble sleeping during the summer in Tromsø, and many homes and hotels put blackout blinds on their windows. Others choose to embrace the endless daylight. They throw parties and stage events such as Tromsø's Midnight Sun Marathon, which doesn't start until 8 o'clock in the evening.

SAMI CELEBRATIONS
The indigenous people of northern Scandinavia are the Sami. They traditionally live a semi-nomadic lifestyle, herding reindeer and sleeping all year round in tents. Tromsø holds a Sami Week every February, featuring reindeer racing and lasso throwing.

WARM AND BRIGHT
It gets bitterly cold in Tromsø. The Sami use the skins of reindeer and the fur of other animals to create natural layers of clothing. The men sometimes wear a ceremonial 'four-winds' hat. Each hat has a distinct pattern relating to the owner's background – a bit like a kilt in Scotland.

FISK

Jørgens RESTAURANT

LARSENS BIFFHUS

ARCTIC FOOD
Many restaurants in Tromsø have arctic-flavoured menus. Whale steak, fish and reindeer meat has been part of the local diet for thousands of years.

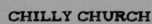

CHILLY CHURCH
Many buildings in Tromsø are made out of wood, including the city's famous old cathedral. Another church, however, holds claim to the grand title of 'Cathedral of the Arctic'. The modern Ishavskatedralen rises up out of the ground like a row of jagged icicles.

AWESOME AURORA

Tromsø is in the heart of the aurora zone. On dark nights an amazing lightshow often takes place in the sky above the city. The freaky phenomenon is known as the *aurora borealis* or 'northern lights'. It is caused by the fusion of cosmic rays, solar wind and magnetospheric plasma, which combine to create a ghostly green glow that dances in the arctic air.

Traditionally, the Sami people believe that the mysterious lights come from the souls of their dead ancestors, and they must be treated with great respect. Even now, some Sami will remain inside when the *aurora* occurs. If caught outside they will stay silent, in case they're taken away by the lights.

STOCKHOLM

SWEDEN Europe

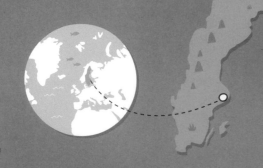

You have to be crazy about the outdoors to live in Stockholm, a watery city made up of 14 different islands and 57 bridges. In summer it hardly gets dark at all – allowing plenty of time to enjoy the city's many parks, boats and beaches. Swedes love their green environment – they even recycle their household rubbish to fuel city buses and taxis.

DARE TO BELIEVE?

If you go on the Stockholm metro never get into a plain, silver carriage. The Silver Arrow, as it's known, is said to be a real-life ghost train! Urban legend says that the spooky train drops passengers at Kymlinge, the Station of the Dead. Luckily, the truth is not quite so scary. Eight silver cars did indeed once roam the metro, but they were all decommissioned during the mid 1990s. As for Kymlinge, there is a real station there, but it has never been open for public use.

VIKING BLING

The Vikings were a fierce bunch with a taste for decadence and bling. Women in the ancient city of Birka, reached by boat from Stockholm's City Hall, wore huge gold and silver neck rings. It was also the done thing for ladies to tie a box to their chest with a knife hanging from it. The knife was used to scoop out earwax!

MAGICAL MIDSUMMER

On Midsummer Eve, the sun's light shines long into the night. Stockholmers flock to the countryside for a magical 'white night' of dancing and merrymaking. Girls pick seven different types of flower and slip them under their pillow. An old Midsummer tale claims that when they drift off to sleep, their dreams will reveal the man that they're destined to marry!

THE DEVIL'S BIBLE

One of the strangest books in the world is kept in Stockholm's National Library. *Codex Gigas* (Latin for 'Giant Book') was made during the 13th century from more than 160 animal skins. The tome is as tall as a baby elephant! If a person sat down today to write out its contents, it would take them five years working continuously day and night – and that doesn't include all the pictures inside.

CRAZY CRAYFISH PARTY

August in Stockholm sees the annual *kräftskiva* (crayfish party). Children make lamps decorated with smiling moon faces and everyone feasts on crayfish, boiled alive fresh from the Baltic Sea. Even the grown-ups wear bibs!

INVISIBLE BIKE HELMETS

Riding a bike is the coolest way to get around Stockholm. As not everyone loves wearing a helmet, a cunning Swedish company invented an invisible version that sits around the rider's neck like a scarf. If the wearer crashes or falls, a fat inflatable hood puffs up around their head in less than a second – just like the airbag in a car.

SWEDEN SOLAR SYSTEM

Only in Stockholm can you ride a glass gondola on the Sun and go shopping on Mars. Spread across the city, the Sweden Solar System is the largest permanent scale model of the Solar System in the world. Different buildings represent the planets and the Ericsson Globe – a wacky, white ball-shaped building – is the Sun.

COPENHAGEN
DENMARK Europe

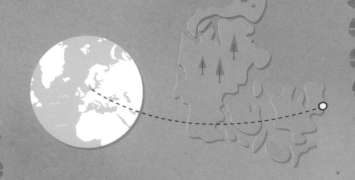

Copenhagen has calmed down a lot since the days of the violent Vikings – a recent report declared that it was the happiest place on the planet! Surrounded by sandy beaches, epic play parks, turreted castles and toy emporiums, it's easy to see why people love to live here.

YOUNG SCIENTISTS
At the waterfront-facing Experimentarium you can surf a giant wave (without getting wet), experience a 5.5-magnitude earthquake (without dying) and perform all sorts of experiments on your family (without getting grounded). The science centre even takes visitors on an elevator ride through the human body.

FAST FOOD
Copenhagen is famous for its fancy gourmet restaurants, but the best meal in town is probably a classic wiener from a *pølsevogn* (sausage wagon). The snack is traditionally washed down with a drink of chocolate milk.

MEET THE STARS
Built in 1642, Rundetårn is the world's oldest working observatory. The observation deck is 34.8m (114.2ft) high, but doesn't have a single step. Instead, a spiral ramp winds all the way up. Cars have been driven to the top, and unicycles are sometimes raced up and down the tower. Nearby, Tycho Brahe Planetarium is Europe's most high-tech portal into the night sky. Amazing 3D films launch visitors into space via a 1,000-square-metre (3,280 square-feet) dome-shaped screen.

HOUSE HUNTER

Copenhagen has some interesting animal residents, including the spitting spider. The creepy creature doesn't make webs. Instead, it sneaks up to its insect prey then squirts it with lethal poison.

PARK LIFE

Walt Disney was inspired to create Disneyland after visiting Copenhagen's Tivoli Gardens. The 720-metre-long (2,362ft) wooden rollercoaster that got Mickey Mouse's creator so excited is still wowing visitors there today. The only amusement park on Earth older than Tivoli is the 431-year-old Bakken. The park is just north of Copenhagen, in the woods of Jægersborg Dyrehave where 2,000 deer roam free. Thrillseekers can run wild there too, taking their chances on 33 belly-flipping rollercoasters, Ferris wheels and drop towers.

GET CONNECTED

LEGO is a combination of the first two letters of the Danish words *leg* (play) and *godt* (well). Denmark is LEGO's birthplace and Copenhagen boasts a flagship store. Shoppers can play well in the creative arena known as the 'Living Room', check out some brain-blowing LEGO models and learn stacks of fun facts.

Did you know that there are 915,103,765 ways to combine six eight-studded Lego bricks?

BYO BUCKET AND SPADE

Most European capitals aren't the place to build sandcastles, but Amager Strandpark is a very impressive exception. The park is a reclaimed island with 4.6km (2.8mi) of sandy beaches and safe swimming lagoons.

TELLING TAILS

The storyteller Hans Christian Andersen is Copenhagen's most famous historical resident. A statue of his Little Mermaid sits by the waterside in the city. She's become a popular character in modern fairy tales, but Andersen's original story didn't have a happy ever after. The mermaid swapped her life under the waves for a human soul and the love of a prince, only to suffer heartbreak and pain. Her bronze twin hasn't fared much better – over the years she's lost an arm, had her head cut off and been covered in paint. She was even once blown back into the sea by an explosion.

EDINBURGH
SCOTLAND Europe

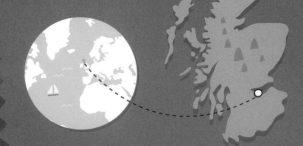

Scotland's capital has a medieval old town and it sits in the shadow of an extinct volcano called Arthur's Seat. Edinburgh loves a party, hosting the biggest arts festival in the world. It rains a lot here, but don't be surprised to see men running around in tartan skirts – kilts are worn for special occasions, but some people wear them all the time.

THE ROYAL MILE

Up until the 17th century, the Scots used different units of measurement to the English. An old Scot's mile is the distance along the Royal Mile from Edinburgh Castle to the Palace of Holyroodhouse. The Scottish version is 205m (672ft) longer than the standard mile. Along a cobbled section of the Royal Mile lies the Heart of Midlothian. Spitting on the heart-shaped mosaic set into the pavement is said to bring good luck!

YUM?

Haggis with *neeps* and *tatties* (mashed swedes and potatoes) is eaten on Burns Night, a supper celebrating Scotland's national poet, Robert Burns. The savoury pudding is made from minced sheep's heart, liver and lungs. The haggis skin is traditionally fashioned from the lining of a sheep's stomach.

EDINBURGH SLANG

In the city, slippers are called *baffies*, a *bairn* is a child and the toilet's a *cludgie*. If someone tells you how *barry* you are, it means you're 'fantastic'. If someone says you're *shan*, things are not so good!

ALL THE FUN OF THE FESTIVAL

The annual Edinburgh Festival brings out everyone's wild side, combining theatre, comedy, art and music into a performance-packed party that lasts for most of August! In 2011, an artist called Dr Bunhead created the world's longest glow-in-the-dark necklace. The super-sized accessory was long enough to wind around the necks of over 100 kids. Another year, four sword swallowers gulped down a stool leg at the same time to set the world record for the 'most sword swallowers swallowing the same object simultaneously'. Definitely not one to try at home!

BATH OF WINE

Mary, Queen of Scots, lived at the Palace of Holyroodhouse in the 16th century. To make her skin more beautiful, she took baths in sweet white wine. The used wine was later bottled and given to the poor. The alcohol was believed to kill germs, parasites and other nasty pests.

HAPPY HOGMANAY

While the rest of the world revels on New Year's Eve, Edinburgh celebrates Hogmanay. The world-famous street party lasts for three days. It includes a torchlight procession, concerts, fireworks and lots of Strip the Willow – a traditional Scottish dance full of energetic spins and twirls.

GREYFRIARS BOBBY

A loyal wee pup called Bobby guards the entrance of Greyfriars churchyard. The story goes that Bobby belonged to a night watchman in the Edinburgh City Police. When the watchman died in 1858, the heartbroken Skye terrier sat pining at his master's graveside. He didn't give up the vigil until his own death 14 long years later.
A local baroness commissioned the bronze sculpture in his honour.

DINNER AT THE CASTLE

Imagine being served a black bull's head for dinner! That's what happened to William, the 6th Earl of Douglas, at a banquet in the Great Hall of Edinburgh Castle in 1440. Unfortunately he did not realize that the head on his plate meant death to the diner – his own head was chopped off straight afterwards.

LONDON
ENGLAND Europe

London is an urban livewire of grand monuments, glowing West End theatres and a headline-grabbing royal family. History has dealt the place its fair share of bad luck over the centuries – deadly diseases, fire, even killer smog – but the city always bounces back. Londoners are made of tough stuff, just like the pigeons that flutter and bob along the busy streets.

NO-GO ZONE
Trafalgar Square used to be more famous for its flocking pigeons than its fountains and stone lions. All that changed in 2003 when the mayor actioned bylaws banning feeding of the birds in the square. Now Nelson can stand on the top of his column without being perched on or pecked!

PORTOBELLO ROAD
On Saturdays, fashionable Londoners shop for antiques at the Portobello street market in Notting Hill. The terraced Victorian houses lining the road are painted in every colour of the rainbow.

CHANGING OF THE GUARD
The Queen of England lives at Buckingham Palace. The grand white building is used to host state visits, royal ceremonies and Her Majesty's famous garden parties. The palace is vast – boasting 775 rooms.

ST PAUL'S CATHEDRAL

PALACE OF WESTMINSTER

BUCKINGHAM PALACE

BATTERSEA POWER STATION
Who would like to live in a vintage power station on the banks of the River Thames? New plans for Battersea Power Station will pop 3,400 contemporary homes inside the iconic building. The plant was designed in the 1930s to look like a cathedral with four sky-high chimneys and wash towers. It is Europe's largest brick building.

CLEOPATRA'S NEEDLE
No single monument captures the love of English history and eccentricity quite like Cleopatra's Needle. The Egyptian obelisk was transported to London in 1877 and planted on Victoria Embankment a year later. A time capsule was hidden in its base. Its contents included cigars, a portrait of Queen Victoria, a railway guide, hairpins, the Bible and pictures of a dozen English beauties of the day.

STATE OF THE ART

Only Londoners can work inside a Cheese Grater, shop in a Stealth Bomber, dine in a glass Shard and negotiate business deals in a Gherkin. These are the names of some of 21st century London's new buildings. Top prize goes to the Walkie Talkie – a skyscraper shaped just like a handheld radio. The feat of engineering quickly earned the nickname 'Walkie Scorchie' after cars parked beneath its reflective, mirrored-glass façade started melting in the sun.

A SLIPPERY SNACK

Jellied eels are London's original fast food. Fished for in the River Thames, the wriggling delicacy were gutted, skinned, chopped and put on the hob to boil with water, vinegar, salt and pepper. Once cooked, they were left to cool and only eaten when the liquid had turned to jelly – slime heaven!

TOWER BRIDGE

A BIRD'S EYE VIEW

Londoners are proud of their city and love showing it off. The London Eye was intended to be a temporary structure to celebrate the Millennium, but the giant Ferris wheel enjoyed such brilliant views it earned a permanent place on the skyline. The other Millennium party piece, the O2 Arena, is the world's largest dome. It is so big, the Great Pyramid of Giza could fit inside it.

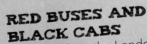

RED BUSES AND BLACK CABS

It is not only at the London Transport Museum in Covent Garden that kids can leap aboard double-decker buses and black cabs. The iconic vehicles zip around the capital at all hours of the day and night, carrying Londoners from A to B. Six and a half million people use the city's buses every single day.

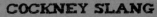

COCKNEY SLANG

Only Londoners born within hearing distance of the chiming church bells of St Mary-Le-Bow Church are true cockneys. East End cockneys are proud of their heritage, and even have their own language. A 'cuppa rosie lee' is a nice cup of strong English tea (always with milk). New phrases come into rhyming slang all the time and they're always fun to guess. Can you translate 'boat race', 'dog and bone' and 'mince pies'?

LONDON

The Tower of London has a dark past. Its 1,000 years of history echo with the crimes and punishments of monarchs, traitors and torturers. The tower is a formidable royal fortress, medieval palace and priceless treasure house rolled into one.

CROWN JEWELS

The royal family's most precious jewels are kept in the Tower under strict lock and key. Millions of tourists ride a travelator past the glittering collection, which includes the world's largest colourless cut diamond. The Star of Africa is a whopping 530.2 carat beauty mounted on the top of a 17th century sceptre used by the Queen for state ceremonies.

BEEFEATERS

Forty Yeoman Warders guard the Tower of London. They live with their families in the Tower and are nicknamed 'beefeaters' because they were originally paid with meat instead of money. Their job is a ceremonial one even though they are all ex-soldiers. Only one beefeater has the special title of 'Raven Master'.

LIFE AT THE ZOO

For 700 years an exotic menagerie of animals lived inside the royal fortress. There were tigers, lions, ostriches, snakes and even an African elephant! In 1252, the king of Norway gave Henry III a polar bear as a present. It was attached to a long chain so it could go fishing in the Thames.

THE RED SEA

In 2014, the empty moat around the Tower of London was filled with exactly 888,248 blood-red poppies – one for each soldier who died during World War One. The dramatic art installation marked 100 years since Britain went to war in 1914.

ROYAL PRISONERS

Hardcore criminals were not the only 'guests' at the Tower of London – several members of the royal family were incarcerated here, too. In the 15th century, the two young sons of King Edward IV were locked up there by their wicked uncle Richard so that he could take over the throne. In 1536 King Henry VIII had his second wife, Anne Boleyn, tried and executed in the Tower – clearing the way for him to marry someone new.

WATERSIDE SPOT

William the Conqueror cleverly had the fortress built on the banks of the River Thames – London's lifeline to and from the outside world. Prisoners sent to the Tower would arrive by boat along the river, entering through Traitors' Gate. Today, the once bloody riverbanks buzz with fun as Londoners enjoy waterfront playgrounds and parks, outdoor art exhibitions, busker shows and street theatre.

TORTUROUS TIMES

Life at the Tower was hardly a bundle of laughs. King Henry I was the first monarch to use the Royal residence as a state prison in 1100, but it was during the Tudor era in the 16th and 17th centuries that things really got nasty. Prisoners were tied on a rack and stretched, or hung by their wrists from the ceiling in manacles, to make them confess their crimes. Heads were chopped off in public executions on Tower Hill, a hillock just behind the fortress.

BLACK RAVENS

Seven jet-black ravens live in the Tower. Legend says that if they ever leave, it will be the death of England. Perhaps this explains why each raven has one wing clipped so it cannot fly very far. The birds eat raw meat and biscuits soaked in blood. Yum!

DUBLIN
IRELAND Europe

Dubliners are a famously friendly bunch who are always up for the *craic*, the Irish word for 'fun'. Their city on the banks of the River Liffey is an energetic place packed full of great museums, galleries and art festivals. Vikings hung out here hundreds of years ago, but today you're more likely to bump into noisy partygoers, lively street musicians and chattering shoppers.

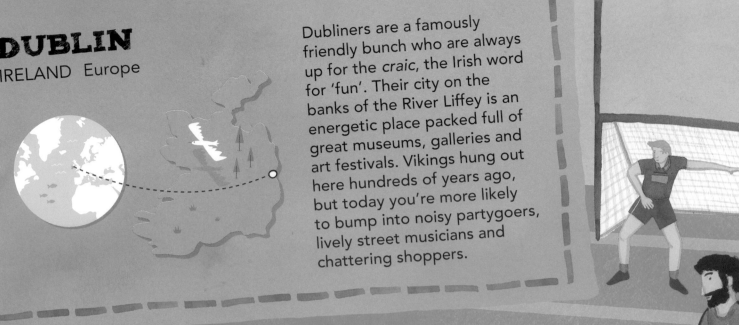

PINT-SIZED
Three million pints (1.7 million litres) of black, frothy Guinness are brewed every day in Dublin's St James's Gate Brewery. Guinness is a much-loved beer with a thick, creamy 'head' on top. In the Guinness Storehouse Museum, visitors are able to stand inside the world's largest pint glass!

THE BOYS IN BLUE
Forget soccer, Dublin kids prefer playing Gaelic football. The fast-paced field game is a high-octane mix of rugby, basketball and soccer. As one of the world's few amateur sports, none of the players, coaches and managers can be paid. The Dubliners' team is known as the 'Dubs' or the 'Boys in Blue'.

SAINT VALENTINE
If you thought the most romantic thing you could do on Valentine's Day was give a soppy card, think again! Hopeless romantics head for a shrine in Whitefriar Street Church. The bones of the real Saint Valentine are believed to rest inside, brought to Dublin from Rome in 1836. Couples pray here and light candles in the hope that their relationship will be a happy one.

THE DUBLIN LION

The first lion to star in the 'roaring lion' logo of Hollywood film studio MGM was a Dubliner. Slats the lion was born in Dublin Zoo in 1919. He later left for the USA, before becoming a world-famous movie star in 1924.

LUCKY LEPRECHAUNS

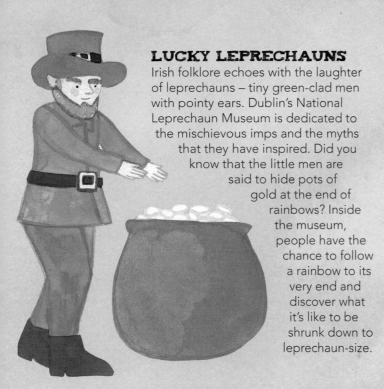

Irish folklore echoes with the laughter of leprechauns – tiny green-clad men with pointy ears. Dublin's National Leprechaun Museum is dedicated to the mischievous imps and the myths that they have inspired. Did you know that the little men are said to hide pots of gold at the end of rainbows? Inside the museum, people have the chance to follow a rainbow to its very end and discover what it's like to be shrunk down to leprechaun-size.

THE BOOK OF KELLS

This national treasure is kept under lock and key in Trinity College Library. Paintings in the sacred gold book are so tiny modern readers need a magnifying glass to study them. Imagine the strain on the eyes of the poor Celtic monks who had to painstakingly write and decorate the pages back in the 9th century!

BOG BODIES

There are some seriously spooky exhibits waiting behind the doors of the National Museum of Ireland. Visitors can pore over perfectly preserved human bodies from the Iron Age, dug up from Irish peat bogs. Stinky peat is dried, cut and burnt like wood in the fireplaces of Dublin homes, but it is also a brilliant way of stopping dead corpses from rotting!

AMSTERDAM
NETHERLANDS Europe

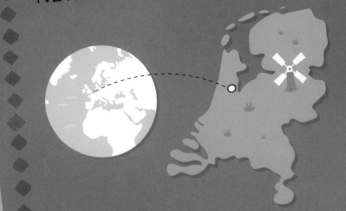

Mellow Amsterdam on the Amstel river delta is one of Europe's most beautiful cities, which might explain why great Dutch artists like Rembrandt and Van Gogh painted it so often. The city streets are peppered with bridges, bicycles, canals and quaint cafés. No one really wears clogs these days, but there are plenty on sale as souvenirs.

SKINNY BRIDGE

Amsterdam is nicknamed the 'Venice of the North' because of its maze of canals crossed by 1,281 bridges. *Magere Brug* (Skinny Bridge) is a drawbridge that opens to let boats through. When it was built in 1691, the passage was so narrow two pedestrians couldn't pass at the same time. Locals claim that the bridge was built by two skinny sisters who lived on opposite sides of the water.

Thirty-eight per cent of all trips in Amsterdam are made by bike!

BIKE-TROPOLIS

Amsterdammers are practically born on bikes! Everyone here, from police officers to postmen, zips around on two wheels – a cycling path even runs through the national art museum, Rijksmuseum. There are more bicycles in the city than residents. Each year 15,000 are fished out of the canals. Locals joke that for every metre (3.2ft) of water, there's a metre of mud and a metre of bikes.

A TRICK OF LIGHT

One winter, a gigantic ghost ship spookily moored itself on the banks of a city canal. Spectators weren't too freaked – it was nothing more than a trick of light! Every November, artists from all over the world come together to create dazzling installations for the Amsterdam Light Festival.

THE HOUSE OF ANNE FRANK

During World War Two, friends in Amsterdam hid a Jewish girl called Anne Frank from the Nazis. The Frank family lived in a secret apartment with a bookcase to conceal the entrance. Anne wrote a diary from her 13th birthday on 12 June 1942, until 1 August 1944 – just a few days before her capture by the Nazis. Less than a year later, Anne died along with her sister Margot in Bergen-Belsen concentration camp. Their father Otto somehow survived and later discovered that friends had rescued Anne's diary. It has since been translated and read in countries all across the globe.

MISSING MASTERPIECES

The theft in 2002 of two paintings worth £25 million from Amsterdam's Van Gogh Museum is on the FBI's top ten list of art crimes. Police found the robbers, but never retrieved the art. Keep your eyes peeled – there's a reward of over £870,000 at stake!

KING'S DAY

On 27 April, more than a million people party on the streets of Amsterdam to celebrate the Dutch king's birthday. Everyone wears orange, stuffs themselves silly with *tompouce* (sweet cream-filled pastries with orange icing), then shops until they drop at a gigantic birthday flea market. Despite the crowds, there are no smelly portaloos at this festival. If you need to go to the toilet you simply look for a moored *plasboot* (pee boat) among the brightly decorated craft lined up along the canals.

DANCING QUEENS

Several tall houses by the canals in old Amsterdam dance – or rather, sag – in all directions. This is because the city is built on soggy marshland. Houses are built on 16m (52ft) wooden stilts that are skewered through the swamp into the firm soil below. Most need five to ten stilts in order to stand up straight, but the Royal Palace on Dam Square has 13,569!

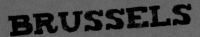

BRUSSELS
BELGIUM Europe

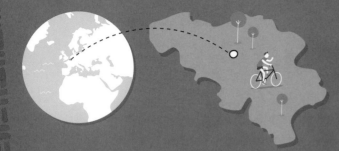

Brussels is one of Europe's most multilingual cities, yet no one speaks Belgian! French, German and Dutch are the official languages, but many more are spoken by the other nationalities living in the metropolis. Brussels is a smart, cosmopolitan centre renowned for its beer, chocolate, sweet waffles and colourful comic book characters.

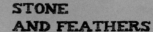

STONE AND FEATHERS

The spooky rooftop gargoyles on the Cathedral of St Michael and St Gudula don't seem to creep out the peregrine falcons that nest at the top of its north tower. Since 2004 the city's falcons have hunted down 44 different bird species. Most days, however, the menu is pigeon for breakfast, lunch and dinner.

TREE OF JOY

Each year on 9 August, seven costumed giants, a troupe of trumpet players and a very large tree parade through the city. The folkloric *Meyboom*, cut down in the forest by *Buumdroegers* (tree carriers) the same morning, is a symbol of joy. Any tree type can be chosen, as long as it is big and planted on the corner of Rue du Marais and the Rue des Sables by 5pm that day. If the tradition is not followed the city is said to be cursed.

COMIC STRIP ACTION

Don't be surprised if you see people laughing out loud as they stroll through the streets of this city. Giant comic strips plaster the exterior walls of dozens of buildings across Brussels. Well-loved characters such as the little blue Smurfs, young reporter Tintin and action heroes Blake and Mortimer were all created by Belgian writers.

17

GET IN LINE!

More chocolate is sold at Brussels' International Airport than anywhere else in the world – 1.5kg (3.3lb) of the stuff is bought every minute! Brussels chocolatier Jean Neuhaus' wife invented the praline in 1912. The chocolate shell had a soft cream centre and was sold in paper cones until Neuhaus came up with the idea of the chocolate box in 1915.

DEEPER ON DOWN

Brussels is home to Nemo 33, one of the world's deepest swimming pools. Divers from all over Europe come to practise in the 34.5m (113ft) diving pool. The school runs courses for everyone from beginners to those looking to learn apnée (the art of free diving without a tank). The underground restaurant has picture windows so that diners can gaze at the swimmers in the deep.

BRUSSELS SPROUTS

Yes, these really do come from Brussels! Sprouts have been grown in and around the city for at least 400 years. The pea-green, nutrition-filled bullets are packed with vitamins and sulphur – which is why overcooked sprouts stink like rotten eggs!

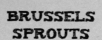

CAUGHT SHORT

Having a wee in public is only allowed in the city if your name is *Manneken Pis*, meaning 'Little Man Pee' in the Brussels dialect, Marols. The tiny bronze statue can be spotted urinating into a water fountain near the Grand Place. Once or twice a year Brussels' famous piddler is even hooked up to a keg of Belgian beer so that he wees ale for the locals to drink! Manneken Pis is very fashion conscious – his clothes are changed two or three times a week. His full wardrobe of around 900 outfits is stored in the Museum of the City of Brussels, along with the original 17th century statue.

PARIS
FRANCE Europe

No city is as romantic as the 'City of Light'. With its famous museums and landmarks, legendary café life and catwalk fashion, Paris is every bit as elegant as people imagine it to be. The city isn't just fabulous however, it's fun too. Think riverside beaches, boats on the Seine, art galleries in recycled train stations, and 18,000 public bikes ready to go on a city spin.

SWEET DREAMS
Paris cooks up some of the finest cakes and pastries on this planet! Local children grow up on chocolate-cream éclairs from L'Éclair de Génie and colourful macaroons from Ladurée tearoom. La Pâtisserie des Rêves is a gourmet cake shop in St-Germain-des-Prés. Its *Paris-Brest*, a choux pastry wheel filled with praline cream created in 1910 for the Paris-Brest-Paris cycling race, is the scrummiest in town.

MUSIC IN THE METRO
Paris' underground stations are filled with music! Live performance is so important to travellers, the metro even employs its own artistic director. Each year thousands of musicians audition for 300 prized spots in the city's underground. Licensed performers are allowed to play in the long corridors, but not on train platforms.

THEFT AT THE LOUVRE
The star of the show at the Louvre is the mysterious *Mona Lisa*, painted by Italian artist Leonardo da Vinci in the 16th century. King Francis I of France bought it to hang in his bathroom. It is the most famous painting in the world, which is why such a scandal erupted when it was stolen in 1911. It took two years for police to track down the robber and recover the masterpiece. Handyman Vincenzo Peruggia was working in the museum when he simply popped *Mona Lisa* under his smock and walked out.

MERCI PARIS!
The French capital gave the world the Cancan dance, plaster of Paris, the Etch A Sketch, and the little black dress courtesy of iconic French fashion designer, Coco Chanel. It began to be known as the 'City of Light' during the 18th century because of the many bright ideas dreamt up by its philosophers, artists and intellectuals. It was also one of the first European cities to get gas streetlights.

AMAZING ARCHITECTURE

Not many buildings are built inside out like the Centre Pompidou. All of its pipes and ducts are brazenly displayed on the exterior of the building. Pea-green pipes carry liquids, yellow carry electricity, and blue carry air. The lifts and escalators are painted pillar-box red. The colour-coded structure houses a huge public library, a music centre and the largest museum for modern art in Europe.

PARK LIFE

When they need a break from the hustle and bustle, Parisians escape to their elegant parks and tree-lined squares. Adults like to flop on a sage-green chair in the Jardin du Luxembourg, while children use sticks to chase boats around the lake.

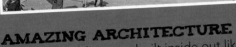

PARIS PLAGES

Life's a beach for four weeks in July and August when 5,000 tonnes (5,511 US tons) of fine golden sand are dumped onto the banks of the River Seine. Parisians play volleyball, lick ice lollies, lounge beneath palm trees on oversized deckchairs and then cool off under de-misters.

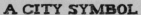

A CITY SYMBOL

When the Eiffel Tower was completed in 1889, Parisians rudely called it the 'metal asparagus'. For 41 years, it was the tallest structure in the world and even now is still the loftiest building in Paris. Queues form every day to climb the tower's 1,665 steps to the top. Over the years, some wacky, brave and downright silly individuals have found other ways of clambering over Gustave Eiffel's creation. On its 100th birthday, tightrope walker Philippe Petit stepped along a very thin wire from the neighbouring Palais de Chaillot to the tower's second level.

PARIS

Paris is not all chic shopping, smart boulevards and supermodel good looks. Dig beneath its stylish surface and you'll uncover a different side to the city. Gruesome Paris is dark, dangerous and begging to be explored. If you dare…

THE CATACOMBS

In 1785, Paris' cemeteries were overflowing. In order to control disease, it was decided that skeletons should be dug up and stored in old quarry tunnels underneath the city instead. For two years, workers trundled back and forth with wheelbarrows, piled high with bones and skulls. The fat of the corpses that had not rotted properly was used to make soap and candles. Today, six or seven million Parisians are packed in neat walls that line the Catacomb tunnels – that's three times more below ground than above!

IT'S A RAT'S LIFE

The only way to get under the skin of the city properly is to roam its sewers. At Paris' Musée des Égouts de Paris, raw sewage flows beneath visitors' feet as they walk through 480m (1,575ft) of gloomy tunnels. If they're lucky, a rat or three might even accompany them! Locals say that there are three rats for every Paris resident above the ground – that makes more than six million!

MONSTERS OF NOTRE DAME

All sorts of scary creatures greet you on the rooftop of Notre Dame Cathedral, but they don't bite. The fantastical birds, dragons and grimacing gargoyles are made from stone. Each one has a drainpipe fitted down its throat to channel rainwater off the roof. When this bestial menagerie was sculpted in the 14th century, it was believed that the creatures would scare off demons. Who wouldn't get freaked out by a beastie like the star chimera? Called 'Stryga', the chimera has wings, horns, a human body and a menacing, waggling tongue!

CATAPHILES AND CATACOPS

Urban adventurers in Paris get a thrill from sneaking into the 280km (174mi) of closed tunnels in the Catacombs. They are called *cataphiles*, and the police who try to stop them are *catacops*. *Cataphiles* sneak underground through manhole covers or underground car parks to put on clandestine theatre performances, dinner parties, discos and cinema showings.

SKINNED AND STUFFED

Paris is famous for its shopping, but not many would expect to go out and buy a stuffed fluffy white rabbit, bird of prey or tiger dressed in human clothing! Shoppers can do just this at Deyrolle, a taxidermy store. The ancient art of skinning and stuffing dead animals has been practised here since 1831. Luckily, today the only creatures used have died of natural causes.

GRAVE TALK

The world's most visited cemetery, Cimitière de Père Lachaise, opened in Paris in 1804. It is as big as 30 football pitches and contains more than 70,000 graves. Lots are eerily beautiful, decorated with carvings and ornamentation. Many famous people have been laid to rest here, but perhaps one of the most haunting tombs belongs to the little known Belgian writer, Georges Rodenbach. A sculpture of the author appears to clamber out of his own grave, clasping a rose in his hand.

BERLIN

GERMANY Europe

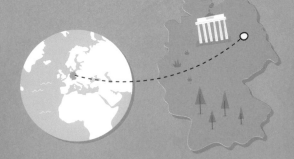

Edgy Berlin is Europe's cool kid. Nine times bigger than Paris, it was once divided by a huge wall and is now one of the most exciting cities on the planet. Berliners love curried sausages, green traffic light men and urban safaris. If you ever visit, don't make the same mistake as US President John F Kennedy who reportedly once said, *"Ich bin ein Berliner!"*, meaning "I am a doughnut!".

RABBITS, RABBITS, RABBITS

At the old Chausseestrasse border crossing between East and West Berlin, 120 brass rabbits hop across the street and pavements. The artworks, inlaid into stone and cement, remember the real-life rabbits that lived in the grassy, 'No Man's Land' in front of the Wall.

In 1979, a mechanic, a mason and their families floated over the wall in a homemade hot air balloon made from propane cylinders and bed sheets.

WHAT A CHAMELEON!

Few buildings have changed their look as many times as Germany's parliament house, the Reichstag. Over the years, the building has been burned down, bombed, reconstructed and flanked by the Berlin Wall. In 1995, avant-garde artist Christo wrapped it in fabric, and then in 1999, world-class architect Norman Foster crowned it with a futuristic glass dome.

FRIEDHOF CEMETERY

BRANDENBURG GATE

CHECKPOINT CHARLIE

MINI MEN

Keep your eyes peeled for Berlin's *Ampelmännchen* – little red and green men showing pedestrians when to 'stop' and 'walk', at city traffic lights. The much-loved hat-wearing figures were first designed in East Germany. These days 'Ampel man' appears on everything from mouse pads and bottle openers to T-shirts, cookie cutters and flip-flops.

In 1983, two men climbed to the top of a tall building, shot an arrow tied to a wire cable down over the wall and zoomed into West Berlin by zip wire.

BEAR-PIT KARAOKE

On warm Sunday afternoons, Berliners flock to an amphitheatre in the city's Mauerpark to sing karaoke! The spot is nicknamed the 'bear pit' because that's what it feels like when you're up there singing in front of the huge crowds that gather to cheer and sway along.

TRABI TOURS

Before the Wall came down, many East Berliners drove a Trabant. The small, smelly car belched out clouds of exhaust fumes. Its bodywork was not metal, but a type of resin containing bits of wool and wood. Today tourists go on Trabi safaris around the capital.

TV
TOWER

In 1962, some old-aged pensioners built a tunnel underneath the wall, hiding the entrance with a chicken coop. The feat took them 16 days.

FAST FOOD

Forget burgers, *currywurst* (pork sausage with tomato sauce and curry powder) is what rocks the fast food stands in Berlin. Berliners eat 127 tonnes (125 US tons) of sausage a day. They even have their own Currywurst Museum. It's painted ketchup-red and kitted out with sausage-shaped sofas.

OUTDOOR ART

The widest remaining section of the Berlin Wall doubles as the world's longest collection of open-air murals. It is called the East Side Gallery. The wall is emblazoned with 101 paintings celebrating the reunification of Germany.

ENGELBECKEN
BASIN

OBERBAUMBRÜCKE
BRIDGE

MUNICH

GERMANY Europe

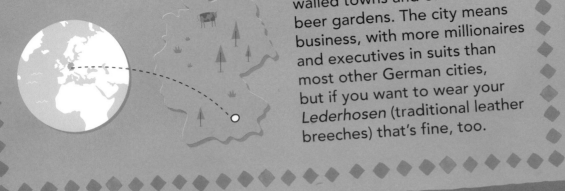

Munich is the capital of Bavaria – a storybook land of princess castles, medieval walled towns and old-world beer gardens. The city means business, with more millionaires and executives in suits than most other German cities, but if you want to wear your *Lederhosen* (traditional leather breeches) that's fine, too.

BREAKFAST SAUSAGE

Munich is the only city in Germany to have its own sausage for breakfast, the Weisswürst. The chalky 'white sausage' is made from minced veal and can only be eaten before midday. The Bavarian way of gobbling up a Weisswürst is to slice off the top, then suck out the insides!

SEPTEMBERFEST?

Munich's world-famous beer festival, the Oktoberfest, is actually held in September. The first event in 1810 celebrated the wedding of Prince Ludwig of Bavaria. Today more than 6 million people drink 6.5 million litres (1.4 million gallons) of beer during the 16-day festivities. Munich's lord mayor starts the proceedings by bashing a wooden tap into a keg and shouting " *'O'zapft is!'* ("it's tapped!") as the beer gushes out.

MUNICH MOTORS

Petrolheads can get excited about the old and the new in Munich. The world's first car, a Karl Benz three-wheeler from 1886, is parked up in the Deutsches Museum. The city is also home to the futuristic BMW World. The main BMW headquarters are located next door and the gleaming chrome tower is designed to look like a 12-cylinder car engine.

VERSATILE VEG

King Frederick the Great of Prussia brought *Kartoffeln* (potatoes) to Germany in the 1700s. In the 18th century they were used to warm up hands, like mini hotwater bottles. The Potato Museum in the city exhibits a host of other surprising uses. In 1755, a man called Johann Ernst Gotzkowsky even decorated his Christmas tree with spuds!

THE SHOW MUST GO ON

The *Schäfflertanz* (Barrel-Makers Dance) can only be seen once every seven years. Twenty dancers, two hoop twirlers, two clowns and a flag bearer perform intricate steps holding green garlands above their heads. The tradition goes all the way back to 1517, when barrel-makers danced through the streets to celebrate the end of the plague in Munich. Don't want to wait seven years? You can see 32 painted life-sized figures do the traditional jig every day in the *glockenspiel* (metal xylophone) at the New Town Hall.

FIVE SEASONS

Munich has four seasons like every one else – and then *Starkbierzeit* (strong beer season). This fifth season rolls out the city's darkest, most intense ales, as well as its mightiest men. The strong men compete at lifting a stone weighing over 250kg (550lb). It's no mean feat – the achievement is the same as holding a Bengal tiger above your head!

RIVER SURFING

There's a massive surfing scene in Munich, but not a beach in sight. Instead urban surfers hang ten in Eisbach Creek. The waves were made when engineers submerged concrete blocks in the water upstream in the Isar River. The blocks were intended to slow the river down, but they also created a rush of swirling rapids. It's fast, it's furious, but at least there's no risk of a shark attack!

KRAKÓW

POLAND Europe

Poland's second-largest city was founded on the defeat of a fire-spitting dragon – tracking down its den on Wawel Hill is a rite of passage for mythology lovers. Kraków is one of the few cities not to have been destroyed during World War Two. The old town radiates out from Rynek Glowny, Europe's largest medieval market square.

THE WAWEL DRAGON

Legend has it that the world will end the day the Wawel dragon bones strung up outside Kraków Cathedral fall. The Wawel dragon is said to have gobbled up young girls in one fiery gulp. Unfortunately one day he wolfed down a lamb stuffed with sulphur, drank half the River Vistula to abate his raging thirst and then burst. Yuk! A statue of Kraków's dragon guards the entrance to his lair. Don't peer down his throat – it really does breathe fire!

LAJKONIK

Lajkonik is a strange wizard of a fellow who trots into town once a year on a giant hobbyhorse. He hits people with his mace for good luck, demands free booty from shopkeepers, and dances a jig with the city mayor on Rynek Glowny. So who is Lajkonik? The medieval hero saved Kraków from invading Tatars, nomadic people originally from Asia. Afterwards he paraded through the city victoriously dressed in a Tatar's glittering glad rags.

SUBTERRANEAN ADVENTURE

Salt was mined at the Wieliczka Salt Mine for 800 years. It is a mysterious labyrinth of underground tunnels, lakes and hollows. Carved chambers hide crystal grottoes, a cathedral and extraordinary salt carvings of the Seven Dwarfs and other fairy tale characters. The mine hosts music concerts and films are shot here, too.

RECORD BREAKER

Travelling on buses and trams in Kraków is a squash and a squeeze – public transport is horribly crowded! In 2011, 229 students from the university decided to cram themselves into a city bus in order to break a world record. The mission was successful, although the bus journey only lasted 57 seconds!

THE KRAKÓW TRUMPETER

It is impossible to forget the time in Kraków. Every hour on the hour a bugle call rings out across the city from the top of a tower at St Mary's Basilica. The *hejnał* is played by one of seven trumpeters. The musicians also work as the city's firemen.

WET MONDAY

Every Easter Monday, boys in Kraków run wild through the city throwing water over passersby. The youngsters come out armed with bottles, buckets, water pistols, plus anything else they can lay their hands on. Girls who get soaked are believed to get married within a year.

DUMPLING FEST

Polish *pierogi* (dumplings) are loved so much in Kraków, they have their own festival. Every August, millions of the tiny moon-shaped parcels are eaten in the city. The myriad filling options range from minced meat, cheese, cabbage, wild mushrooms and mashed potato to sweet wild berries from nearby forests and even chocolate!

GHETTO HEROES

During World War Two between 1.1 million and 1.5 million people died at Auschwitz, a death camp set up by the Nazis near Kraków. Ninety per cent of people killed were Jews, brought here by train from all over German-occupied Europe. Many were from the Kraków Ghetto, a part of the city where Jews had to live. Each person was allowed no more than 100 grams (3.5 ounces) of bread a day and 200g (7oz) of sugar a month. On Plac Bohaterów Getta a memorial by architects Piotr Lewicki and Kazimierz Latak remembers the city's 'Ghetto heroes'. Seventy larger-than-life bronze chairs are peppered across the big public square.

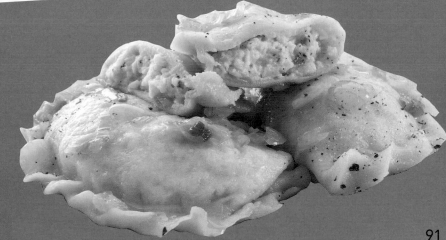

PRAGUE
CZECH REPUBLIC Europe

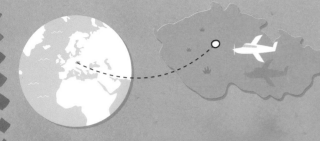

Prague, capital city of an independent Czech Republic since 1993, is known by many names – it's the 'Paris of the East', a 'City of 100 Spires', the 'Golden City' and even the 'Mother of Cities'. The city is fabled for its church spires, cobblestone streets and enchanting fairytale castle.

FRED AND GINGER

There's a curious, curved building on the waterfront in Prague. The Dancing House is made of two towers that twist and lean into each other. World-famous architect Frank Gehry nicknamed it 'Fred and Ginger' after the famous dancers Fred Astaire and Ginger Rogers.

THE BEARDED MAN

A carved stone head looks out across the embankment near the St Francis Church. The effigy is known as the 'Bearded Man'. Locals say that if the water of the River Vltava rises up high enough to lick the man's hairy chin, the river will flood.

CHARLES BRIDGE

For 500 years the Charles Bridge was the only way to cross the River Vltava. Today it is a hot spot for musicians and street performers, tourists and locals. Rub the shiny statue of St John of Nepomuk to ensure your return to Prague – and thank your lucky stars it was not you who was chucked off the bridge in 1393. A cross and five stars mark the exact spot where the saint met his grisly end.

WEIRD CHEESE

Headcheese (*Tlačenka* in Czech) is not what you think it is. The savoury nibble is actually cold, jellified meat made from a boiled pig's head. Slices of headcheese are traditionally eaten in Prague with vinegar, raw onion and bread. Scrummy!

THE WORLD'S LARGEST CASTLE

Prague's fairytale fortress is epic in its proportions. Work started on the official residence of the President of the Czech Republic way back in the 9th century. The complex is listed in the *Guinness Book Of World Records* as the largest ancient castle in the world. It is so immense seven football pitches could fit inside it.

A RICH MAN'S DRINK

Feeling rich? Nip into Prague's Alchemy Museum to buy a bottle of drinkable gold. They say that a few sips will help you stay young forever (or at least very healthy). The tonic is made from 77 different herbs that sap up gold from the soil around them. The ancient art of alchemy was huge in Prague in the Middle Ages. Harry Potters across the city did everything they could to turn minerals into gold and discover the secret of the fabled elixir that guarantees eternal youth.

BEWARE, GIANT BABIES ON THE LOOSE!

The space-age babies crawling up the outside of Prague's TV Tower have eerie, barcode faces. They are the creation of rebel sculptor David Černy, whose daredevil sculptures are dotted all over the city. He's even designed a fountain showing two men peeing – visitors can send a text message to it to make it move.

HOW ASTRONOMICAL!

The huge medieval clock on Prague's Town Hall doesn't only tell the time, it also shows the months, zodiac signs and positions of the Sun and Moon. The clock is so beautiful a legend has sprung up around it. The story goes that city councillors had the eyes of the poor clockmaker burnt out with red-hot pokers so that he couldn't make another for anyone else.

VIENNA

AUSTRIA Europe

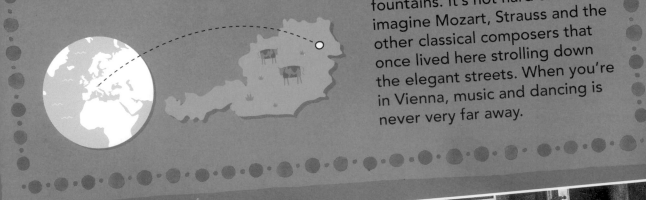

Vienna is a real beauty. The city is laced with grandiose squares, dazzling palaces and dancing fountains. It's not hard to imagine Mozart, Strauss and the other classical composers that once lived here strolling down the elegant streets. When you're in Vienna, music and dancing is never very far away.

AMAZING TREASURE

The wonders stashed inside Vienna's Imperial Treasury are truly flabbergasting. There's a giant narwhal tooth said to be the horn of a unicorn, an ancient bowl which might be the Holy Grail and a thorn believed to come from the crown of Christ. The most dazzling treasure has to be the world's largest cut emerald, made for Hapsburg King Ferdinand III in 1641. It is 2,860 carats – as heavy as half a bag of sugar.

THE MAESTRO

Ludwig van Beethoven lived in Vienna. The classical composer became deaf at the age of 31, but astonishingly he continued to write music for another quarter of a century. He used tools to help him feel vibrations instead of sound. An interactive exhibit at Vienna's House of Music shows people what it would be like to compose in silence.

TALL ORDER

The south tower of St Stephan's Cathedral is the tallest in the city – and that's official! A 14th century law declared that no building in the old town of Vienna could exceed it in height. The north tower should have matched the south's lofty 136.4m (447.5ft) step for step, but it was never finished.

FUN AT THE FAIR

Vienna's Ferris wheel started twirling in 1897 and has not stopped since – it is 64.75m (212.43ft) tall and for 65 years was the highest wheel in the world. One of its 15 gondolas is furnished with crystal glasses for a romantic dinner for two.

THE WORLD'S MOST FAMOUS CHOCOLATE CAKE

If Prince Metternich's court chef had not been taken ill one day, the world would never have had the delicious *Sachertorte*. The famous creation was cooked up in 1832 by a 16-year-old apprentice chef called Franz Sacher. The cake is cut into three layers then sandwiched together with apricot jam and iced with velvety chocolate. Every coffeehouse in Vienna now has it on their menus.

TAKE ME TO THE BALL!

The ball season waltzes into the city just before Christmas and runs right through to March. Anyone can buy tickets to the 450 or so themed dances that are put on each year. The ladies wear long flowing ball gowns and the men don dapper tails or tuxedos. There is an Opera Ball, an Engineer's Ball, a Coffeehouse Owner's Ball, a Doctor's Ball, a Flower Ball and even a sweets-themed Bonbon Ball! At midnight one of the guests is elected to become Miss Bonbon. Afterwards her weight in sweets is calculated and given to charity.

SNOW IN THE CITY

Viennese mechanic Erwin Perzy was tinkering with a light bulb in 1900 when he accidentally invented the snow globe. At first he used semolina to make the snow inside, but he refined this as time went on. Perzy snow globes are made of glass, but their snow recipe is still top secret today. Each miniature scene inside is carefully painted by hand.

AIRS ABOVE THE GROUND

The Spanish Riding School in Vienna is the oldest classical riding school in the world. Its stables, right in the city centre, house around 70 snow-white Lipizzaner horses. The creatures are known for their extraordinary prancing moves. Riders train for years to achieve 'airs above the ground', where all four of the horse's hooves lift off the floor at the same time.

MOSCOW
RUSSIA Europe

There is no need for an alarm clock in Moscow – the sound of early-morning street cleaners scraping snow off the pavements is the wake-up call in this cold, ancient city. Luckily, there are *chapkas* (fur hats with ears) and cabbage rolls to keep residents warm through the icy winters. And when summer arrives, Moscow rushes out to enjoy the eco-friendly paths and playgrounds of Gorky Park.

KNOCKERS AND SPITTERS

Muscovites are a superstitious lot – there's no shaking hands across the threshold and definitely no offering bunches of flowers containing an even number of blooms (that's only for funerals and dead people). To ward off bad luck, city dwellers knock on unpolished wood or – watch out – spit over their shoulder three times.

BILLIONAIRE CAPITAL

More billionaires live in Moscow than any other city in the world. Many hang out in Moscow City, the city's financial district. Futuristic high-rises loom over the men and women below. At 339m (1,112ft), the Mercury City Tower is the tallest skyscraper in Europe. After dark, Moscow's elite go to see the Bolshoi ballet or dine at Turandot, an opera-themed restaurant which cost millions of rubles to furnish and decorate.

WEDDING CAKES

After World War Two, Soviet dictator and leader Joseph Stalin ordered the construction of seven skyscrapers. The skyscrapers were designed to help make Moscow appear just as modern as cities in the United States of America. The tiered buildings, with their wide bases and central spires, were nicknamed the 'Seven Sisters'. They looked just like traditional wedding cakes.

NUTS ABOUT SQUIRRELS

Keeping a squirrel as a household pet is the latest craze to hit the capital. Poachers steal Siberian red squirrels away from city parks where they live thanks to feeders fixed on trees and filled with nuts, fruit and other food. Once trapped, the bushy-tailed rodents are sold on as pets. Bagging one is not to be advised – the fine for stealing a squirrel is 20,000 Russian rubles.

MOSCOW METRO

Moscow's metro system is vast and often very beautiful. Stations like Komsomolskaya are decorated with painted friezes, arching columns and chandeliers. Some nine million people use the metro every day, which is the equivalent of the entire population of Sweden hopping aboard! It can be tricky for foreigners to find their way around – the names of its 196 stations are only signposted in the Cyrillic alphabet.

TOP SECRET!

METRO 2

No one really knows if the Metro 2 exists or not. The mysterious subway system is said to run underneath the regular metro. It was apparently built for Stalin, connecting the Russian leader's house with a secret underground 'city' in southwest Moscow, complete with a nuclear bombproof bunker for 15,000 people.

TRANS-SIBERIA

Only in Moscow can you hop aboard a train and stay on it for 10,214km (6,346mi). The trip from Moscow to Pyongyang in North Korea is the world's longest single train ride – the record-breaking, Trans-Siberian journey takes 7 days, 20 hours and 25 minutes.

DOGS IN SPACE

Moscow's Monument to the Conquerors of Space – a soaring rocket-shaped monument celebrating Russia's amazing space programme – is just like a *matryoshka* (Russian doll). A cosmonautics museum is tucked inside the monument. Inside that are two very special dogs, preserved in glass cases. Belka and Strelka were the first animals to go to space and return alive. They made their historic voyage in the spacecraft Sputnik 5 on 19 August, 1960 with one rabbit, two rats, forty-two mice, several insects and some plants.

MOSCOW

Krasnaya Ploshchad, or Red Square, is not red. 'Beautiful Square' – the old Russian translation of its name – is far more accurate! Over the centuries the massive car-free swathe of cobblestones has been a market place, a military parade ground, a festival stage, a book fair, a concert hall, a dance floor and an ice rink. In the 17th century, rebels and mutinous palace guards were brought here to have their heads chopped off.

STREET MELODIES

There is no finer spot in the whole of Moscow to drum up an audience. Crowds gather in Red Square to clap along with street musicians and watch shows by performance artists. Some buskers go to extreme measures to get noticed! One artist even took off all his clothes and nailed himself to the cobblestones – until the police arrested him.

KREMLIN

Red Square was built to separate the Kremlin from the rest of the city. The citadel is the world's largest medieval fortress and home to the Russian government. It is from the Kremlin that autocratic tsars, communist dictators and modern-day presidents have ruled the nation – for better or worse.

WORLD'S LARGEST BELL

The Tsar's Bell in the Kremlin grounds is so gigantic people can actually hang out inside it! The bronze creation was commissioned in 1733 by a niece of Peter the Great and was once used as a chapel. The 'doorway' was created after a fire in 1737 shattered part of the bronze. The chunk that fell off weighs 11 tonnes (12.13 US tons) – the same as two elephants!

ASSUMPTION CATHEDRAL

This 15th century church behind the Kremlin's high walls is Moscow's oldest building. In 1812, the French emperor, Napoleon Bonaparte had the cheek to use it as a stable for his horses after invading the city. Upon retreating, he ordered the entire Kremlin to be blown up. Luckily rain ruined the dynamite and saved the citadel.

MODERN MUMMY

The deceased founder of the Soviet Union, Vladimir Lenin, is the world's most modern mummy, lying in his own mausoleum beside the Kremlin wall. Lenin died from a stroke in 1924. He wanted to be buried next to his mother in St Petersburg, but the queue of mourners to see his body was so enormous the state had the communist leader pickled instead.

SHOP 'TIL YOU DROP

Behind the souvenir stalls, tourists and brides in meringue dresses posing for photos sits GUM, the state department store. Not all Muscovites can afford to come here. Its prices are known for being notoriously high, yet the huge, beautiful glass-topped building from 1893 is always packed with shoppers. In Soviet times, the top floor housed Section 100, a secret clothing store open only to top officials. Queues to buy hard-to-find goods sold in the rest of the shop stretched outside across Red Square.

ONION DOMES

The nine colourful domes of St Basil's Cathedral are an unforgettable part of the Russian skyline. The church was built between 1555 and 1561, under orders from Ivan the Terrible, a powerful and violent Grand Prince of Moscow. Eight chapels symbolize Ivan the Terrible's eight assaults on Kazan, a rival Tatar town 640km (400mi) down the Volga River. The final chapel was added later to house the tomb of Saint Basil. Despite its grand appearance from the outside, St Basil's is very cramped inside. Its small chapels are linked by a maze of old, stone galleries.

PRIPYAT

UKRAINE Europe

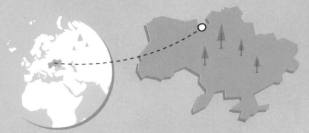

Why would an entire town flee their homes? This is what happened in 1986 when the Chernobyl nuclear power station exploded, covering the area in radioactive dust. Only now are tourists returning to explore the infamous ghost city of Pripyat. Wildlife is also flourishing once more, while engineers continue working to make the plant safe.

CHERNOBYL TOURS

Guided tours of Chernobyl are starting to bring life back to the place, but special passes are needed to enter the Exclusion Zone. Visitors can see the ghost city of Pripyat where school classrooms sit eerily empty and clocks still show the time of 11:55 – the moment that the electricity in the city was cut off.

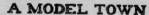

A MODEL TOWN

Imagine having a town built especially for you! That is what it was like for workers at the Chernobyl nuclear power plant. Life was good for the 50,000 people living in Pripyat, 3km (1.8mi) away. Salaries were high, food shops were well stocked and there were good schools and recreational facilities. Children were looking forward to trying out the Ferris wheel in the town's newly built fairground. The attraction was just about to open when Chernobyl's reactor number 4 exploded.

RED FOREST

Radiation killed the green leaves and brown bark of pine trees in Chernobyl's surrounding forests – leaving naked red trunks behind. The trees then died, but bizarrely they have not decayed, creating a very spooky landscape.

DANGER ZONE

After it exploded, Chernobyl spewed out a massive cloud of nuclear dust. The radiation meant that it wasn't safe to stay anywhere within a radius of 2,800 sq/km (1,700 sq/mi) of the power plant. This area is called the Exclusion Zone. It will continue to be too dangerous to inhabit for another 20,000 years. Experts still can't agree on how many people have lost their lives. Two plant workers perished in the blast and 29 more died a few days later in hospital from acute radiation poisoning. No one knows how many have died or will die of cancer caused by the radiation.

THE ELEPHANT'S FOOT

This is said to be the single most dangerous object on the planet. It is made out of solidified black lava produced from the melting core of reactor number 4. The lava lump is shaped like an elephant foot and hides in the base of the reactor. Minutes in its company will cause death a few days' later.

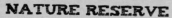

TWO-WEEK SHIFTS

The Chernobyl power plant is being decommissioned, but it's a big job to make the ruined reactor safe. The 7,000 people who work here are only allowed to stay in the Exclusion Zone for two weeks at a time. They work five hours each day at the plant and pass through a special radiation detector machine when they leave.

DEADLY TOMB

The original concrete casing built over Chernobyl's exploded reactor to stop it leaking was only made to last 30 years. Now the world's engineers have come up with a new one that will be good for 100 years. Because the reactor site is so dangerous, they are assembling 29,400 tonnes (32,400 US tons) of steel and 680,000 bolts at a distance. When the mammoth arch is ready, it will be rolled over the old casing to seal off the deadly reactor.

NATURE RESERVE

Several villages in the Exclusion Zone were buried because radiation levels were so high. But mountains of new clean soil have been dumped in the area, and flora and fauna – free of human predators – is now thriving! Wolves, wild boar, birds and elk share the wild nature reserve.

THE FIREMEN

At Chernobyl fire station a monument remembers the heroic firemen who fought the raging flames immediately after the explosion. The fire burned for two weeks. It was eventually extinguished by helicopters dropping 5,000 tonnes (5,600 US tons) of sand, lead, clay and acid onto it.

ISTANBUL
TURKEY Europe

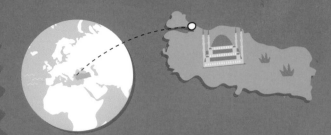
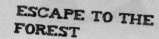

Europe and Asia meet on Istanbul's ancient streets. The skyline twinkles with minarets and mosques, church spires and grand palaces. Over the last 2,000 years, the Greek, Persian, Roman, Byzantine, Venetian and Ottoman empires have all helped make today's Istanbul one of the most dazzling places on the planet.

ESCAPE TO THE FOREST

Istanbul is home to over 14 million people. To escape the crowds, families head to Belgrade Forest in the north of the city. The former royal hunting ground is now a lovely leafy retreat, perfect for picnicking, playing games and bike riding. Deer, wild boar, snakes and even wolves live in the 5,500 hectares (13,590 acres) of woodlands. Local schools go on trips to Atatürk Arboretum, a living museum where 2,000 plants grow and terrapins swim in the lake.

THE PALACE BENEATH

The Basilica Cistern is a massive underground structure designed to store water. It was built almost 1,500 years ago and then forgotten about for centuries! The cistern was cleaned up and opened to the public in 1987. It's a spooky, cavernous realm. Visitors walk past eerie Medusa heads then tiptoe along wooden platforms. Ghostly, pale fish circle silently in the pools below.

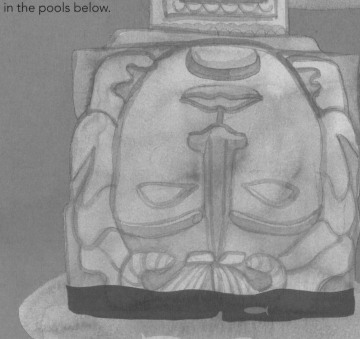

TRANSFORMERS

As control of the city swapped from Christian to Muslim rulers over the centuries, many churches were converted to mosques. The beautiful Aya Sofya started as a Christian cathedral in 537, became a mosque between 1453 and 1935, and is now a museum.

NAME GAME
The city was first called Byzantium by the Ancient Greeks, Nova Roma (New Rome) and then Constantinople by the Romans, who made it the capital of their empire in 330 AD. It only officially became Istanbul in 1930, after nearly 500 years of Turkish rule.

TOTALLY BAZAAR
Chaos and colour rule supreme in Istanbul's Grand Bazaar, a busy and bustling place where hidden doorways and secret lanes reveal stalls laden with trinkets. There are lamps waiting to be rubbed and carpets that look good enough to fly on. Canny shoppers drink tea, compare prices and then haggle for a bargain.

TINY TOWN
Miniatürk, the world's largest miniature park, is a scale model of Istanbul. It features 105 famous structures from Istanbul and around Turkey, all at a teeny 1/25th of their actual size. The sprawl of paths, pools and mini monuments sits on the banks of the Golden Horn estuary.

DAWN CHORUS
At the last count, there were 2,944 active mosques in Istanbul. Every morning the city wakes up to the sound of muezzins (servants of the mosque) making their call to prayer. The famous Sultanahmet Mosque is also known as the Blue Mosque. Its six minarets stand out amongst the forest of towers that make up Istanbul's skyline.

ISTANBUL

Istanbul is spread across a pair of continents, sandwiched between several seas and split by a waterway. The Bosphorus Strait runs through the very heart of the city, separating Asia from Europe.

CROSSING CONTINENTS

Every July, over 1,600 people take part in Istanbul's famous Bosphorus race. Contestants swim 6.5km (4.04mi) from Asia to Europe in an extraordinary intercontinental competition. Luckily, shipping is stopped during the event.

GOLD CHAIN

The Golden Horn is an estuary that joins the Bosphorus Strait as it meets the Sea of Marmara, creating the peninsula around the oldest part of Istanbul. When the city was the capital of the Byzantine Empire, a huge chain was pulled across the mouth of the estuary to prevent enemy ships from entering and attacking the naval fleet moored inside.

TWO-WAY TRAFFIC

The Bosphorus Strait is a strange stretch of water – currents flow along it in both directions at the same time! Surface water travels out of the Black Sea, through the strait and eventually into the Mediterranean Sea, but a deeper current simultaneously flows the other way, from the Sea of Marmara back into the Black Sea.

GOLDEN

THE GRAND BAZAAR

EUROPE

HIPPODROME OF CONSTANTINOPLE

SEA OF MARMARA

ISTAN BALL

Istanbulians are football crazy! The Turkish National Premier League features five teams from the capital, including Fenerbahçe and Galatasaray. Fiercely contested matches between these two football giants are known as the *Kıtalar Arası Derbi* (Intercontinental Derby). Fenerbahçe hail from the Asian part of the city while Galatasaray are based on the European side.

END OF THE ROAD

Istanbul was once the last stop on the 6,437km (4,000mi) Silk Road. The ancient route connected China and India to Europe. Everything from silk and spices to knowledge, drugs and disease passed through the city crossroads.

EUROPE

ST ANTHONY OF
PADUA CHURCH

GALATA
TOWER

HORN

THE BOSPHORUS STRAIT

TOPKAPI
PALACE

BASILICA
CISTERN

AYA
SOFYA

ASIA

THE BLUE
MOSQUE

SUBMARINE TRAINS
An underwater railway tunnel runs beneath the Bosphorus Strait, providing a vital link between Europe and Asia. The idea of a rail tunnel was first suggested by the Ottoman ruler, Sultan Abdülmejid, in 1860. The new line was opened in 2013. Now that it's complete, a train could potentially run all the way from London to Běijīng!

DARING DOLPHINS
Nicknamed the 'street children of the Bosphorus' by marine biologists, three species of dolphin live dangerously in the strait that divides Istanbul. The mammals can often be seen surfing the bow waves of huge boats in one of the world's busiest shipping lanes. Harbour porpoises and short-beaked common dolphins migrate between the Sea of Marmara and the Black Sea, but around 60 larger bottlenose dolphins live permanently in the Bosphorus.

ROYAL RECREATION
On hot summer days, people like to jump on a ferry to the Princes' Islands, just off the coast of Istanbul. This calm stretch of the Sea of Marmara is a sun-lover's playground, lined with sandy coves and beaches. The islands were once a place of exile for princes and sultans.

ATHENS
GREECE Europe

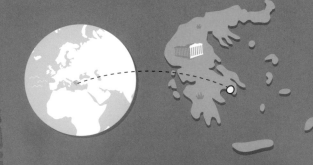

Nowhere conjures up the great age of mythical monsters and ancient gods quite like Athens. Greece's huge, hectic cosmopolitan city is one of the most historic in the world – as well as being Europe's oldest capital. It is, however, ultra-modern, too. Beneath the Acropolis there are buzzing markets, outdoor cafés and a vast pedestrian zone.

DRAMA IN ATHENS

Athenians have a great sense of drama, but then they did invent the theatre! Ancient Greek tragedies penned thousands of years ago continue to be staged in spectacular amphitheatres such as the Odeon of Herodes Atticus and the Epidaurus Ancient Theatre, south west of the city.

DRACONIAN LAW

Democracy was born in Athens during the 7th century BC. For the first time ever, a man called Draco decided to write down the city's laws. The Greek writer, Plutarch, later said that these laws were 'written in blood, not ink'. Every crime, be it stealing a cabbage or worse, was punishable by death!

RUNNING MAN

Dromeas is a modern statue of a man sprinting down Vassilissis Sofias Avenue, one of Athens' most glamorous streets. To create the illusion that the runner is moving at speed, Athenian sculptor Costas Varotsos made his 12m (39ft) tall work of art out of stacked sheets of broken glass.

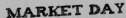

MARKET DAY

The city's central food market is called Dimotiki Agora. A trip to the glass-topped market hall plunges shoppers headfirst into the noise, chaos and mayhem of Athens' urban life. It can be a gory experience – locals head there to buy skinned rabbits and slimy cow intestines. Dimotiki Agora is also the finest place in town to purchase chunks of freshly butchered pig to make traditional *souvlaki* (skewered meat).

GRAVE CONCERNS

Noisy Athens is so jam-packed with people, buildings, traffic and historic landmarks, the city is running out of space to bury its dead. Graveyards are overcrowded and plots have to be recycled. Bodies are buried for three years, then the bones are dug up, washed in wine, popped in a box and moved to a communal 'ossuary' (a storeroom for bones).

MOONLIGHT MAGIC

The ancient Parthenon on top of the Acropolis is one of the most copied buildings in the world. It is at its most stunning during the August Moon Festival, the brightest night of the year. Over 100 famous sites and monuments all across Greece are opened up to celebrate the full moon. Athens' Acropolis can only be admired from a distance, however – it has to be kept closed after dark for safety reasons.

PORT SIDE

The rows of tankers, ferries and cruise liners filling the quays at Piraeus, Athens' humungous port, are quite something to behold. Eighteen million passengers sailed through here in 2014 – the equivalent of the populations of both Hungary and Sweden hopping aboard! The biggest ever sea battle in history was fought at Piraeus between Athens and Persia in 480 BC. More than 1,000 ships and 200,000 men took part.

OLYMPIC FEATS

Athens' most famous invention, the modern Olympic Games, kicked off in 1896 in the Panathenaic Stadium. It is the only stadium in the world to be built entirely in white marble. Before the Olympic torch leaves Greece on its world tour at the start of each new Olympic Games, a 'flame handover' ceremony is held here.

ROME
ITALY Europe

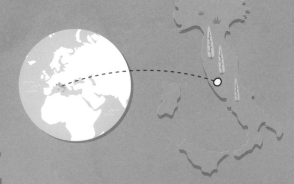

Sprawling and noisy, Rome wears its incredible imperial past on its sleeve. There's no need to visit museums to see ancient relics and architecture – a wander through the streets and you'll step back thousands of years to a time when the Roman Empire ruled Europe and beyond. Romans today are fashionable, family-oriented and proud of their glorious city.

BEAUTIFUL VIEW

For a picture-perfect view, local Romans peep through the keyhole at the front of the Priory of the Knights of Malta. They are rewarded with the sight of St Peter's Basilica in the nearby Vatican City. St Peter's dome rises majestically above terracotta buildings and distinctive umbrella pine trees.

COLOSSEUM

This is Rome's tourist hot spot. Four million people a year come to gaze at the ancient amphitheatre and imagine the wild animal hunts, bloody gladiator bouts, ceremonies and shows that once took place inside. Romans viewed the sacrifice of humans and animals as entertainment. During the show celebrating the opening of the Colosseum in 80 AD, more than 5,000 animals were killed. The sand in the arena was often dyed red to disguise the blood stains.

ALL ROADS LEAD TO ROME

Romans love to buzz around their beautiful city on scooters. Navigating the car-clogged roads on two wheels can be risky. But then again, Romans take their cars and scooters to church each year to be blessed. In March, they zoom to the Festa di Santa Francesca Romana to celebrate the patron saint of drivers.

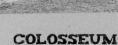

NO FIBBING!

La Bocca della Verità (the Mouth of Truth), carved in stone in the porch of the church of Santa Maria in Cosmedin, is no ordinary sculpture. Since the 17th century, the wild-haired face has earned a reputation as a lie detector. Tell a lie while your hand is placed in its mouth and you risk having it bitten off.

TREVI FOUNTAIN

Rome has over 2,000 stunning fountains, but the magnificent Trevi sculpture in travertine stone is definitely the most famous. Oceanus is shown riding a shell-shaped chariot led by Tritons and two sea horses. Visitors who love Rome should turn their back to the fountain and throw a coin over their left shoulder into the water, to ensure their return to the city. People say an average of £2,100 gets chucked in daily.

WHEN IN ROME...

...do as the Romans do and eat both heartily and healthily. Local cuisine features simple ingredients such as lamb, cod and vegetables flavoured with pork fat, garlic and herbs. Specialities include *bucatini all'amatriciana* (hollow pasta in a tomato and pork cheek sauce) and *carciofi alla romana* (stuffed artichokes).

SPOOKY RECYCLING

Capuchin monks had an interesting take on interior design. They kitted out a cemetery in the crypt of their church, Convento dei Cappuccini, with bones! They used femurs for chandeliers, skulls to build archways and the bones of 4,000 of their departed brothers to deck out the macabre monument to death. Some skeletons they left whole – and dressed.

DUMPED AT BIRTH

Everywhere in Rome you can spot images and souvenirs featuring a she-wolf suckling two little boys. These are the twins Romulus and Remus. Legend says that they were abandoned at birth and left to drift in a basket on the River Tiber. But they were saved by a she-wolf. Once grown-up, they decided to build a city on the spot where the wolf had found them. Unfortunately the brothers quarrelled and Romulus killed Remus, naming the city Rome after himself.

VATICAN CITY

VATICAN CITY Europe

The Vatican City is both a city and a country at the same time. Many languages are spoken there – and yet it is smaller than the average golf course. It has museums and chapels, but no schools. The few children who live here cross an invisible border each day to attend school in Rome in Italy.

SISTINE CHAPEL

The frescoes by Michelangelo on the ceiling of the Vatican's Sistine Chapel cover the same space as one-sixth of a football pitch. It took the Italian painter and sculptor four years to paint. There are more than 300 figures in the paintings that Michelangelo created whilst standing on scaffolding – not upside down as many people think!

WORK, REST AND STAY

The Vatican City is the only country in the world that does not give you citizenship, at birth. To become a citizen, you must work in the Vatican City. When your job ends, your citizenship does, too.

SECRET BALLOT

There is no other vote quite like it in the world – to elect a new Pope, cardinals meet in the Sistine Chapel to cast secret ballots. At the end of the day smoke puffs out of a tiny chimney on the chapel roof. Black smoke means that a Pope has not yet been elected, white smoke means that he has.

CIVIL ADMINISTRATION BUILDING

RAILWAY STATION

LAST RITUAL

In the past, when a Pope died, the Vatican's *Camerlengo* (Chamberlain) is believed to have knocked three times on the Pope's forehead with a silver hammer and calls out his name. When there was no reply, he proclaimed that the Pope was officially dead.

ST PETER'S BASILICA

St Peter's is easily the biggest, richest and most spectacular church in the whole of Italy. At least 60,000 people can fit inside for mass while thousands more regularly gather on the vast square in front of the building for outdoor services. So many people have kissed or rubbed the statue of St Peter on their way into the Basilica, the toes on his right foot are completely rubbed away.

EXPRESS SERVICE

The Vatican City doesn't have a king or a government. Its ruler is the Pope whose head appears on Vatican City coins and postage stamps. The postal service is so super efficient that Romans living down the road in Italy nip across the border to post their letters there.

POPEMOBILE

If you spot a white, glass-sided vehicle motoring along the few streets in the Vatican, it could be one of the Pope's Popemobiles. The cars are specially designed to help the Pope stay visible to large crowds. Some are open-topped, others have bulletproof windows. The high security modifications were introduced in 1981 after someone shot at Pope John Paul II.

VATICAN MUSEUMS

VATICAN GARDENS

ST PETER'S BASILICA

THE SISTINE CHAPEL

ST PETER'S SQUARE

WORLD'S OLDEST ARMY

The Swiss Guard is the world's oldest army still in active service – its distinctive striped blue and gold uniform harks back to Renaissance times. The Guard's 110 soldiers really do come from Switzerland and their job is to protect the Pope. They are armed with a deadly half-axe, half-spear weapon called a halberd.

GREAT ESCAPE

A secret passage called Passetto di Borgo links the Vatican with Castel Sant'Angelo on the banks of the River Tiber. During the Sack of Rome on 6 May, 1527 Pope Clement VII used it to escape from the bloodthirsty soldiers of the Roman Emperor Charles V. It saved his life – most of his Swiss Guard were brutally murdered on the steps of St Peter's.

VENICE
ITALY Europe

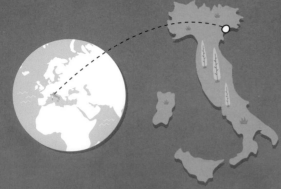

Venice is Europe's most famous labyrinth. Exploring this small Italian city, built from razor-thin alleyways and romantic canals dotted with gondolas, is just like playing an adventure board game. Tourists vastly outnumber the local Venetians, but that just adds to the charm.

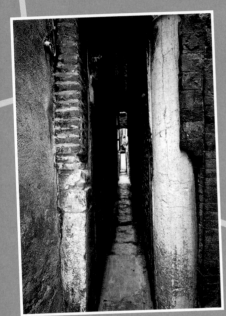

FLOATING CITY

The construction of Venice was extraordinary. Wooden planks were laid on submerged islands in the Adriatic Sea to create a magical floating city of 118 islands and hundreds of canals. There are no proper roads for cars – just a twisting maze of pedestrian *calli* (lanes), *campi* (squares) and *fondamente* (canal-side alleys) understood only by locals. The narrowest street, *Calletta Varisco*, is just 53cm (21in) wide!

ACQUA ALTA

There was just one hitch with the Venice build – its foundations were not solid. The city is slowly sinking. Rising tides of seawater often flood the town, drowning squares and cutting off roads. Sirens go off across the city when *acqua alta* (high waters) are expected. Venice hopes its streets will be kept dry by 2018 when the massive MOSE barrier will kick into action. The barrier will have 78 gigantic steel gates to control the amount of seawater entering the Venice lagoon.

CAMPO SAN POLO

GRAND CANAL

CHIESA DI SAN VIDAL

GALLERIE DELL' ACCADEMIA

CIAO!

Ciao is used all over Italy and Europe to say 'hi' and 'bye'. The word was born in Venice – a city with a local dialect that mixes Italian, French, Portuguese and Greek together to make Venetian.

BASILICA DI SAN MARCO

One glance at the spangled spires, domes and glittering mosaics of the Basilica di San Marco in Venice's busy central square makes it easy to see why Venetians are so proud of their city. The church was built to house the remains of the body of Saint Mark, smuggled back from Egypt by Venetian merchants in a barrel of pork fat in AD 828. The basilica's treasury also houses the arm that Saint George slayed the dragon with!

BRIDGE OF SIGHS

Originally Venetian footbridges had no steps, so that horses could cross easily. The city has over 400 bridges, but the most romantic is the Bridge of Sighs. Legend has it that lovers can enjoy eternal love if they kiss on a gondola beneath the bridge at sunset, while the bells of San Marco chime.

GONDOLAS AND GONDOLIERS

The gondola is the traditional mode of transport used to get around Venice's narrow waterways. Eight types of wood are used to make the 280 pieces which form the hull alone. There are around 400 gondolas in use, licensed like taxis to carry passengers. At the helm of each is a gondolier, dressed in a striped shirt and a straw hat. In 2010, Venice issued a license to its first ever female gondolier.

RIALTO BRIDGE

SANTA MARIA FORMOSA

BASILICA DI SAN MARCO

ST MARK'S SQUARE

BRIDGE OF SIGHS

DOGE'S PALACE

VENICE

Since pre-Christian days, people have been getting up to all sorts of shenanigans to celebrate the approaching end of winter. The spectacular Venetian Carnevale, held each February, is the most flamboyant celebration of them all.

FLIGHT OF THE ANGEL

The Flight of the Angel opens Carnival on the central square. A beautiful woman shoots down a zip wire into the square from the top of San Marco's bell tower, scattering rose petals on the crowd as she 'flies'. Once the celebration is declared open, masked parties, balls, posh dinners and beauty pageants are the order of the day for anyone wearing a costume.

PIAZZA SAN MARCO

Café society is classy and elegant on Piazza San Marco – except during Carnival when the central square is transformed for weeks on end into a heaving mass of masked revellers posing and preening as they promenade. Theatre shows, jugglers, clowns, circus acts, musicians and other crazy street life add to the raucous atmosphere.

PARTY TIME

Over the centuries all sorts of strange entertainments have been cooked up to excite the carnival spirit. Live dogs have been fired from cannons and bulls (and once, even a rhino) have been let loose to chase runners through the city streets. Thankfully today the party revolves around masks, music, masquerade balls and other more civilized merriment.

AN EXCUSE TO BE NAUGHTY

Everyone wears a mask during the Venice Carnival, a tradition enjoyed by Venetians since the Middle Ages. Historically, covering the face gave the wearer a great excuse to be naughty! Masked nobles and commoners could dance together, forbidden lovers could meet in public, and gamblers were free to win and lose money without being recognised. Until 1797 Venetian nobles wore masks for several months of the year.

DOCTOR DEATH

The most famous mask of all is Doctor Death or *Il Medico della Peste* (Plague Doctor). The costume dates from the 17th century when doctors tried to treat Plague victims, donning long ugly gowns and strange face pieces in an attempt to protect themselves from infection. These curious figures wander the streets carrying a stick during Carnival, looking like terrifying black birds with huge white beaks.

THE MEN BEHIND THE MASKS

The art of Venetian *mascherari* (mask makers) is awe-inspiring. Along the canals plenty of souvenir shops sell cheap ceramic masks, but nothing compares to the real deal. An authentic Venetian mask is crafted by hand in papier-mâché or leather, then decorated with gold leaf, feathers and sparkly gems. There are seven different types of masks. Some cover the entire face, whilst others simply hide the eyes and nose. Decoration ranges from the plain ghost-white *Volto* to the richly adorned *Colombina*, a women's half-mask that drips in gold, silver and crystals.

MADRID

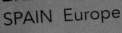

SPAIN Europe

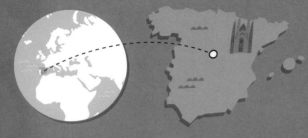

Madrid is like a big child that buzzes with energy and never wants to go to bed. This capital city – Europe's highest at 650m (2,133ft) – is a party town! There are green parks, fun shopping malls, and countless bars, restaurants and clubs. It's a crazy, captivating place to be. As everyone says, 'if you're in Madrid, you are from Madrid'.

WORLD'S OLDEST RESTAURANT

Madrid's Botín restaurant has been open since 1725. Its signature dish is *cochinillo asado* (roast suckling pig) – cooked whole in a wood-fired pizza oven. As in most restaurants, children are welcomed, but there's no kids menu. Youngsters in Madrid are used to enjoying the ceremony and tastes of a hearty meal and happily sit at the table for hours with their family and friends.

LONG DAYS, LATE NIGHTS

Being a kid in Madrid takes stamina. Many children are up by 7.30am for the walk or bus ride to school. Lessons run from 9am until midday, with a break for lunch and a *siesta* (nap). Children might walk home and back for this, or stay at school if their parents both work. Lessons then continue from 3pm until 5pm. Back home, once their homework is done, the warm evenings are spent playing outside in the street or in parks like the huge Casa de Campo. The Spanish eat very late, so even very young children often don't go to bed before 10 or 11pm on a weekday.

FROM EGYPT WITH LOVE

In1960, Spanish archaeologists helped save temples and other monuments in Egypt from flooding during the construction of a dam. To show their gratitude, Egypt dismantled the ancient Temple of Debod during 1972 and then sent it to Madrid, stone by stone. That's an impressive thank you gift!

KITTY CITY

People from Madrid are called *Madrileños* or *los gatos* (the cats). The animal nickname was coined in 1083 when medieval Madrid was occupied by the Arabic Moors. Alfonso VI tried to free the city, but couldn't, until a young super-agile soldier scaled the high city walls like a cat and dropped a rope down for the other men to climb up.

REAL MADRID

Footie fans go to heaven in Madrid, home to the world's most successful soccer club. According to research carried out by the club in 2015, Real boasts 450 million fans around the world! Home matches are played at Madrid's Santiago Bernabéu stadium, a hot spot for football fans on Saturday afternoons.

WINGING IT

A curious naked winged man crashes headfirst into the roof of 3, Calle de los Milaneses. Far from being a classical 'fallen angel', the *Accidente Aereo* (Air Accident) is by contemporary artist Miguel Ángel Ruiz. The sculpture shows a figure who left tiny rural Madrid only to find an enormous city on his return 10,000 years later!

PALACIO REAL

Madrid's royal palace has 2,800 rooms, but only 50 are open to the public. It's impossible to forget the time in the dazzling Salón de Gasparini – 215 of the 700 clocks in the royal collection tick-tock the hours away here. The walls of the chamber are covered in silk with real gold and silver embroidery.

DECIDEDLY FISHY!

Madrid is nowhere near the sea, but a taste of the ocean awaits at the MercaMadrid. The wholesale fish market is the biggest in Europe! The market sells a mind-boggling 220,000 tonnes (242,000 US tons) of fish a year – including shoals of Spanish bluefin tuna.

BARCELONA

SPAIN Europe

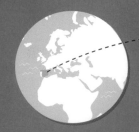 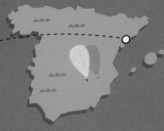

Barcelona is one of Europe's coolest cities. It offers sun, sea and sand, and has always been on the cutting edge of fashion and design. The modern Catalan architect, Antoni Gaudí, gave the metropolis its incredibly distinct look. Thanks to Gaudí, the structures, surfaces and buildings of Barcelona glitter with dazzling ceramic mosaics.

CHIP OFF THE OLD BLOCK

Barcelonians have always made handsome, handmade pottery and ceramics. Today shoppers love to wander the city's markets and back alleys on the hunt for traditional artisan workshops. The first important building Gaudí designed in Barcelona was for a rich ceramic factory owner. Casa Vicens is covered in colourful mosaics called *trencadis*, made from pieces of broken tile. Almost all of Casa Batlló, a house Gaudí remodelled in 1904, is mosaic-covered, too. The eye-catching building is said to resemble the humped back of a dragon or dinosaur!

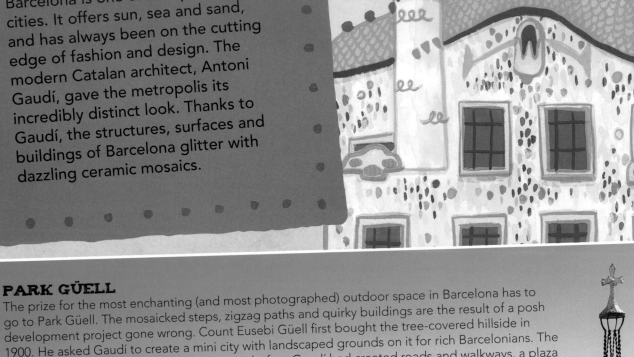

PARK GÜELL

The prize for the most enchanting (and most photographed) outdoor space in Barcelona has to go to Park Güell. The mosaicked steps, zigzag paths and quirky buildings are the result of a posh development project gone wrong. Count Eusebi Güell first bought the tree-covered hillside in 1900. He asked Gaudí to create a mini city with landscaped grounds on it for rich Barcelonians. The ambitious project was later ditched, but not before Gaudí had created roads and walkways, a plaza and two gatehouses in his own unique style.

LA RAMBLA

No boulevard in Spain is more talked about than La Rambla! Barcelona's famous main street is crammed with flower stands, souvenir sellers, bars and a constantly revolving parade of people from all corners of the globe. Not many realise however that La Rambla is actually made up of five streets all joined together. This is why it is also called the plural – Las Ramblas. In the early evening half the city emerges to stroll, eat and hang out on the tree-lined strip.

OLYMPIC CHANGE

Barcelona's golden beachfront is world famous, but it has only been around since 1992! The city used to have its back turned towards the sea, lining its coast with industrial buildings and factories instead. When Barcelona won its bid to host the Olympic Games, organisers decided to transform the entire area. The old buildings were knocked down, two beaches were improved and five brand new ones were created. Now the seaside is an essential part of Barcelona life – a place to play, swim and while away the weekends.

WORK IN PROGRESS

La Sagrada Familia is a gigantic stone church, rising from the ground like a cluster of colossal stalagmites. The pillars propping up the vast interior resemble trees and the church will eventually have 18 spires. Currently however, it only has eight. Although the first brick was laid in 1882, Gaudí never got to see his vision completed. Over a century later, La Sagrada Familia is still under construction. Given that the Great Pyramid of Giza in Egypt only took 20 years to build using ancient tools, this is quite a delay!

HUMAN CASTLES

The Catalan people can't get enough of beautiful architecture. In fact, they even like to build towers or *castells* (Catalonian for 'castles') out of human beings! The sport is called *castellars* and Barcelona has its own club. Huge crowds gather to watch it performed on Plaça de Sant Jaume to celebrate La Mercè, a festival held towards the end of September, honouring the city's patron saint. People stand, carefully balancing on top of each other, creating a tower that can reach up to ten storeys high. Grown-ups are too heavy for the higher levels, so children, clad in crash helmets, teeter at the top.

LISBON
PORTUGAL Europe

Living in Europe's only capital city blessed with ocean-facing beaches, lucky Lisbonites enjoy sensational surf and marvellous marine cuisine. It's the kind of place you never want to leave, yet the golden age of exploration began right here, with Portuguese ships sailing west, off the edge of the known world.

LORD OF THE PIES

All Portuguese cuisine is delicious (especially the seafood), but in the capital a mysterious little pie is the undisputed top of the taste pops. *Pastéis de Nata* – cloud-soft, sweet-as-you-like custard tarts – are a Lisbon sensation. The café at Antiga Confeitaria de Belém sells 16,000 handmade, warm *Pastéis de Nata* a day. The sweet treats were invented by Catholic monks at the city's Jerónimos Monastery in Santa Maria de Belém. Their 180-year-old recipe is a guarded secret, only disclosed to three chefs at a time.

JURASSIC PARK LIFE

Lisbon is surrounded by nature parks. Cabo da Roca in Sintra-Cascais Natural Park is mainland Europe's westernmost point, known as the place 'where the land ends and the sea begins'. Real dinosaur tracks can be seen wandering up the chalky south cliff behind the park's Praia Grande, as though the mighty monsters have just waded ashore. The fossilised footprints are 100 million years old, and are believed to belong to Megalosaurus and Iguanodon.

DISCOVERY ZONE

In medieval times, the Atlantic was known as *Mare Tenebrosum* (Sea of Darkness). The Portuguese helped light up the modern map during the Age of Discovery in the 15th and 16th centuries, producing explorers like Vasco da Gama, who left Lisbon to become the first European to reach India by sea. Padrão dos Descobrimentos (Monument to the Discoveries) on Lisbon's Tagus River celebrates these adventurous achievements.

FADO
SAD-O

Lisbon has its very own soundtrack – a traditional style of music called *Fado*, which features people playing guitars and mandolins. A *fadista* sings a story over the top. The tale is usually a sad one about love, mourning or loss.

SURF AND SOCCER

With the Atlantic Ocean lapping at their door, fun-loving city dwellers regularly hit the seaside at weekends or after school. Central Carcavelos is popular with local kids, who spend hours playing beach football on its flat golden sands. Praia do Guincho beach, just north of the city centre, is famous for its amazing sunset and great breakers for surfing.

PLACE OF WONDER

The Jerónimos Monastery is an amazing 500-year-old Gothic landmark, carved out of pale stone. Beauty lies in every intricate detail. The buildings are decorated with some of the most awesome gargoyles and scary beasts in Europe, but there are also astonishing scalloped arches, tiered cloisters and columns twisted with stone vines and leaves.

HILL BUSTERS

Lisbon's nickname is A Cidade das Sete Colinas (The City of Seven Hills). Bright canary-yellow trams wobble and screech up and down the sloped streets, which sometimes sit on different levels. A bizarre lift has been also erected to help residents get around. The Elevador de Santa Justa was designed by an apprentice of Gustave Eiffel (who built the Eiffel Tower). The lift is now so famous it has become a tourist attraction.

MARRAKESH

MOROCCO Africa

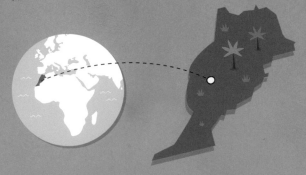

Hot, hectic and heaving with history, Marrakesh is a head-spinner of a city. The mighty Atlas Mountains look down upon a metropolis that's brimming over with North African magic and mayhem. The streets buzz with Moroccan steam rooms, maze-like markets and public squares full of snake charmers and performers.

HIDE AND SOUK

There are *souks* dotted all around the Djemaa El-Fna square. These outdoor markets go back to the days when North African Berber tribes came to the city to trade. The *souks* are tucked away in a warren of tiny alleyways that get mind-blowingly busy. Mysterious magic shops rub shoulders with communal bakeries and artisan studios.

PRIVATE PALACES

Marrakesh is full of marvellous *riads* – traditional Moroccan houses – where the garden is on the inside! The *medina*, or walled quarter of the city, has many fine *riad* mansions. Many have fantastic flat rooftops too, from where it's possible to see the Atlas Mountains. It's hard to imagine in such a sweltering city that people go skiing in those hills!

SECRET GARDEN

Marrakesh might be nicknamed the 'red city', but Jardin Majorelle splashes some big beautiful blobs of blue and green into the mix, too. The 1-hectare (2.5-acre) botanical garden, an oasis of calm amid the chaos of the city, was created by French painter Jacques Majorelle in the 1920s and 30s. The blue he used to paint the buildings is so uniquely bright that it's now named after him – *bleu Majorelle*.

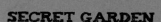

ON YOUR BIKE

Stubborn donkeys, wandering tourists and horn-happy car drivers all clutter Marrakesh's streets, but it is scooters that rule these roads. Driven by everyone from kids to old ladies, the vehicles zip fearlessly in and out of the traffic. The bold bikers include a group of free-spirited young women, nicknamed the 'Kesh Angels'. The group dress in traditional outfits, customised with pop art colours and modern flourishes, such as love heart sunglasses.

A DAY IN THE LIFE OF THE DJEMAA EL-FNA

As dawn breaks and the sun clambers over the 12th century clay walls of the medina, the old town is painted in shades of ruby and rust. Traders lead laden donkeys into the Djemaa El-Fna and set up stalls selling everything from fish and freshly squeezed orange juice to spices, shoes and souvenirs. It's a kaleidoscope of colour.

According to one translation, the 1,000-year-old square's name means 'the assembly of death' and it was certainly the scene of public beheadings in ancient times. Nowadays it's a manic marketplace where all of Morocco seems to be squished into one arena. By late afternoon the square bustles with hawkers, performers, Berber and Tuareg tribesmen, tourists, henna painters, snake charmers, monkey trainers, street dentists and pickpockets.

As the sun slides behind the 70m (230ft) tower of Koutoubia Mosque and dusk descends, the *muezzins* begin calling Muslims to evening prayer. The lights come on and the increasingly crowded scene is cast anew. In the semi-darkness, hot food stalls crank up their coals, creating a flavour-filled fog. Snail soup, a Moroccan delicacy, is sold all over the square. The big brown snails are cooked in a broth bursting with flavours, including thyme, pepper, citrus peel, aniseed and mint. Customers chatter and laugh over cups of sweet mint tea.

The cooking smoke spirals up into the air and the night buzzes on. *Chleuh* dancing boys and storytellers entertain the locals, while visitors gawp at magicians and stare at the astonishing array of traditional medicines on offer. It's the end of just another amazing day at Djemaa El-Fna.

CAIRO
EGYPT Africa

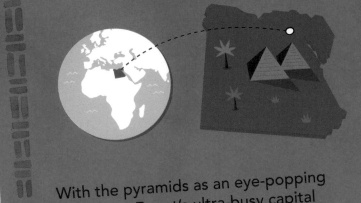

With the pyramids as an eye-popping backdrop, Egypt's ultra-busy capital sprawls across a site that's been populated for thousands of years. Grand Cairo is actually two cities, split in half by the Nile river. The modern metropolis of 'Downtown' Cairo occupies the east bank, while old Giza sits pretty on the west, full of churches, mosques and bazaars.

MEET AND EAT
In Cairo, people love to eat out. Corner cafés are full of men sipping tea, smoking *hookahs* (water pipes) and chatting about politics, while kids run around munching charred corn cobs and falafels from street stalls. A staggering 353 new restaurants opened up in Cairo during 2014 – almost one a day. To show that they're full, Egyptians often place their right hands across their tummies.

TUTS AND CURSES
Cairo's Egyptian Museum houses mummies and all sorts of dazzling artefacts from the Valley of the Kings, an ancient burial site further upstream along the Nile. It is also the current resting place of Tutankhamun's famous golden death mask. He is the best known of ancient Egypt's pharaohs, because of the excitement caused by the discovery of his treasure trove of a tomb in 1922. The so-called 'Curse of the Pharaohs' claims doom will descend on anyone who disturbs the burial chambers of the kings. There's little evidence for this, but museum workers did get into hot water in 2014, after allegedly dropping King Tut's death mask, breaking his beard off and gluing it back on wrong…

OLD AND EVEN OLDER
Contrary to popular belief, Cairo wasn't a historic hangout for pharaohs. The ancient Egyptian capital was actually a place called Memphis, located 20km (12.5mi) away on the Nile's west bank.

SOME STRINGS ATTACHED

For over 50 years the Cairo Puppet Theatre has staged free shows for local kids most Thursday and Friday nights in Downtown Cairo. The performances are conducted by skilled master puppeteers. The entertainers speak in Arabic, but the shows are so vibrant and colourful anyone can enjoy them.

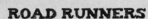

ROAD RUNNERS

In Egypt, the weekend starts on a Friday. Recently on Friday mornings Cairo's usually car-clogged streets have been invaded by a new breed – runners. Despite the lack of green spaces and the city's hectic roads, running has become very popular in recent years. Some participants in a recent marathon were so worried about traffic however, they competed wearing American football style padding!

SUPER SOUK

A busy bazaar now bustles on the site that once housed the Saffron Tomb – a burial place for the Fatimid caliphs (the founding fathers of Cairo). The stalls of the Khan el-Khalili sell everything from souvenirs to jewellery and chandeliers.

LIFE GIVER

The Nile once nourished one of the planet's oldest civilisations in ancient Egypt and now flows through 11 modern countries. Cairo is the last and most famous city on its entire 6,671km (4,145mi) length. A little further north, the river braids into a broad delta and then drains into the Mediterranean. In ancient times, hippos and Nile crocodiles lived on Cairo's riverbanks, but they're long gone. The Nile monitor still remains however – a cold-blooded, dragon-like lizard that grows up to 2m (6.6ft) from tip to tail.

CAIRO

Across the Nile from Cairo's modern skyscrapers, lies the Giza Plateau – one of the most famous historical sites in the world. The three pyramids and the Great Sphinx still baffle historians and archaeologists alike. How were they possibly built in ancient times, and why?

TALL ORDER

At 147m (482ft), the Great Pyramid of Giza was the tallest building on the planet for over 3,800 years. Initially it had smooth sides, but the outside layer has gradually peeled away. Even so, the pyramid has truly stood the test of time. It is the oldest of the Seven Wonders of the Ancient World and the last one still standing.

MISSING MUMMY

Pharaoh Khufu's tomb lies inside the Great Pyramid. There are two main chambers, originally reached via a secret swivel door and a series of very narrow passages, which once featured sliding slabs to foil tomb raiders. The lower room, mistakenly called the Queen's Chamber, was probably only meant to house a statue. The upper room, reached via a Grand Gallery, is the King's Chamber, which contains a sarcophagus (stone coffin). It is eerily empty. The site has been raided and robbed many times, so the royal body may simply have been stolen, but some theories suggest he's lying hidden elsewhere in the pyramid.

THE GREAT SPHINX

At the end of a causeway leading from Khafre's temple is the famous Sphinx, an almighty limestone lion with a human face and a pharaoh's headdress. The enormous face is thought to be that of Khafre, but it's hard to tell because the nose has been smashed off. The Sphinx's Arabic name means 'Terrifying One' or 'Father of Dread'.

A TRIO OF TRIANGLES

Three large pyramids form the plateau's famous horizon. The Great Pyramid of Giza (sometimes called the Pyramid of Khufu) is the biggest of the lot. The smaller two belong to Khufu's son and grandson. Ancient Egyptians had a death cult obsession and a fascination with the afterlife. Khufu was the first pharaoh buried here. His pyramid contains 2.3 million heavy stone blocks. According to a graffiti tag scribbled by builders in the upper levels, it was finished by 2560 BC.

A PERPLEXING PUZZLE

Nobody can agree about the Giza Plateau. Are the pyramids just titanic tombs for the pharaohs, or do they double as a huge sundial, a complex calendar or a symbolic staircase to the stars? These issues have been debated for centuries, but there are still more questions than answers. This is what makes the place so fascinating.

THE GRANDSON'S PYRAMID

The smallest of the main structures is Menkaure's Pyramid. When the burial chamber was entered in 1837, a beautiful decorated sarcophagus was discovered. Unfortunately it was lost when it sank to the bottom of the Mediterranean Sea whilst it was being taken to England to be studied.

THE SON'S PYRAMID

The second largest structure at Giza is Khafre's Pyramid. Although smaller than his father's, it is built on higher ground and is much more elaborate. Inside the burial chamber is a pit that probably held jars filled with the pharaoh's organs, removed before he was mummified. Khafre's heart would have been left inside his body, but his brain would have been thrown away, because Egyptians didn't realise the organ's importance.

KHUFU'S PYRAMID

The oldest structure is also the most mysterious – a third chamber called the Old Tomb lies beneath Khufu's pyramid. It's empty, but a dead-end passageway wormholes away from it. Strange narrow shafts branch off from the two main chambers too, possibly to allow Khufu's spirit to travel to the stars. In 2014, the shafts were explored by robots. Several little doors were discovered – believed by the ancient Egyptians to be gateways between the real world and the afterlife.

TIMBUKTU
MALI Africa

Timbuktu is often described as a mysterious doorway to the end of the world, but it is a real city populated by very real people. The ancient city of gold basks on the red-hot southern rim of the Sahara Desert. In Timbuktu, the streets are made of sand and motor vehicles are massively outnumbered by donkeys and camels.

MAGNETIC GOLD

The mystique surrounding Timbuktu has existed almost as long as the city has. In the 14th century it was a super-rich capital of the Mali Empire, with so much gold that stories of its wealth spread right around the world. Countless explorers and treasure hunters risked death in the desert trying to find the remote city.

BEATING THE HEAT

Timbuktu's temperature can top 54 degrees Celsius (130 degrees Fahrenheit). To survive this sweltering heat, every house keeps some water in a big, unglazed jar. As the hours pass, the pottery slowly leaks and the evaporation cools the air. At bedtime, many people sleep outside to enjoy the cool, night air. Many animals only come out at night, too. Aardvarks bury themselves in the sand during the heat of the day, then forage around the city when it gets dark, looking for ants and beetles.

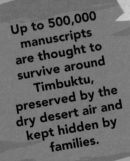

Up to 500,000 manuscripts are thought to survive around Timbuktu, preserved by the dry desert air and kept hidden by families.

SAHARA SCHOOLS

Timbuktu was once an oasis of education in a desolate desert. Amazing mosques and *madrassas* (Islamic teaching centres) built from mud and timber are still standing. They have been operating as schools for seven centuries. Astronomy, mathematics, medicine, history and law were all taught at the ancient universities of Timbuktu, and texts were brought here from Cairo, Baghdad, Persia and elsewhere. Now, after recent political problems, less than 25 per cent of Mali's kids can read or write. Unfortunately it's even worse around Timbuktu, where few Tuareg children get any schooling.

CARAVAN CAPERS

Timbuktu grew up around a well on an ancient caravan route. Years ago, up to 10,000 camels would take gold, ivory and salt along this trail, right up to the Mediterranean, in a procession known as the Azalai. Trucks now transport rock salt along unsealed roads, but the Tuareg people still use camels. The Azalai is one of the last Saharan caravan routes still in use.

LIFE IN THE SANDPIT

For some people in Timbuktu the desert is, quite literally, knocking on the door. In the older parts of the city, doorways can be several metres lower than the street. Sand from the Sahara blows in and raises the level of the ground, slowly burying the houses.

WELL NAMED

A popular story claims that the city got its name from the word *tin* (well) and an old Tuareg woman called Buktu. Buktu was known for her honesty, so Tuareg travellers would leave their valuables with her when they went away. When asked where their belongings were, they would simply say, "I left them at Tin Buktu". Another theory suggests that the city's name comes from the Berber word *Buqt*, meaning 'far away'. *Tin-Buqtu* translates loosely as 'a place almost at the other end of the world'.

CATS AND WITCHES

Cats in Timbuktu are not blessed with nine lives. The unfortunate felines run wild throughout the city and are very much mistrusted. Timbuktu's cats have long been associated with shape-shifting witches and evil genies. The local folklore is so strong, it's even become a tradition for young boys to kill and sometimes eat the animals.

DAKAR
SENEGAL Africa

Dakar is spread across the very western tip of Africa. In this city, hawkers sell street food to businessmen working in skyscrapers, and horse-drawn carts queue up next to flashy sports cars. It's all hustle and bustle until a goat ambles across the road, bringing everything to a noisy standstill. Senegal's capital is an explosion of chaos and colour.

DAKAR DELICACIES

Breakfast in Dakar is likely to involve croissants and pastries – a reminder of centuries gone by when Senegal was colonised by the French. The city's favourite meal is known as *ceebu jën* or *thiéboudienne*. Fish chunks are stuffed with herbs, then served with rice and vegetables. Locals sit around a bowl and eat it using their right hand. The meal is washed down with *jus de gingembre* (ginger juice) or *bouyi*, a drink made from the fruit of the baobab tree.

LAYEN MAUSOLEUM

AFRICAN RENAISSANCE MONUMENT

GRAND MOSQUE

PRESIDENTIAL PALACE

MUSEUM OF AFRICAN ARTS

CAP MANUEL

BREAK CHANCERS

In contrast to its chaotic streets, Dakar's sandy beaches and surf breaks are surprisingly quiet. The best beaches are to the north, but only a few wave-riding visitors venture this far. Proper boards are hard to come by and locals can often be seen surfing on salvaged pieces of wood or plastic.

BIG BABIES

Humpback whales spout and splash off the peninsula around Dakar between September and November, when many of the females have calves in tow. Animal lovers go to Cap Manuel to try and sneak a peek at the big mammas. The whales venture into the warm water close to the coast to feed their babies up and get them ready to face the open ocean.

BEST DRESSED

Young or old, rich or poor, Dakarians are snazzy dressers. Both men and women commonly wear lovely long-flowing robes called *boubou*. Women dress incredibly colourfully, even when doing chores and carrying baskets around on their head.

WACKY RACES

Dakar has become famous for its far western location. For almost 30 years an eccentric event called the Paris-Dakar Rally saw cars, trucks and motorbikes race 10,000km (6,200mi) from France to the city. Entrants crossed the Sahara Desert, facing all sorts of perils on the way. The race moved to South America in 2009, but it's still known as 'The Dakar'.

HOUSE OF SLAVES

Between the 16th and 19th centuries, the Atlantic slave trade saw millions of Africans transported in terrible conditions from the continent's west coast to work on plantations in the Americas. The Maison des Esclaves (House of Slaves) on Gorée Island, 3km (1.9mi) off the coast of Dakar, is a memorial to these people. The Door of No Return is a bleak opening on to the water that symbolises how the Africans were torn away from their homes and families forever.

MISSING THE POINT

The African Renaissance Monument towers at the top of one of Dakar's twin seaside hills. At 49m (161ft) high, the statue is the tallest in Africa, looming even higher than New York's Statue of Liberty. It shows a woman beside a man holding a child pointing west, symbolising the start of a great new era. When it was first unveiled in 2010 however, the bronze family raised a few eyebrows. Critics said that the monument was too expensive and religious groups complained that the woman's skirt was too short.

ADDIS ABABA
ETHIOPIA Africa

Ethiopia's capital is a city of clashing contrasts, where shepherds urge animals past high-tech tower blocks. *Addis Ababa* means 'new flower' in Amharic, the country's official language, and sections of this rapidly growing metropolis certainly are blooming. Poverty, however, remains a terrible reality – an estimated 60,000 kids live on the city's streets.

ULTRA RARE TREAT

In Addis Ababa, Easter is celebrated not with chocolate eggs, but with a meat feast. It is traditional for Christians to go vegan for 56 days before Easter Sunday, refusing to eat any meat or animal products. Once the holiday begins, they celebrate with dishes containing uncooked ox and goat meat. A favourite is *kitfo* – raw minced beef marinated in herbed butter and spices.

RESIDENTS OF THE SKY

Humans might own the streets in Addis Ababa, but birds definitely rule the sky! Many large species swoop and wheel overhead, including thick-billed ravens, yellow-billed kites and hooded vultures. The vultures may not look pretty, but they provide a service to the city's exploding population. Large numbers of people create a large amount of waste – vultures are more than happy to scavenge amongst it and help clear up.

BORN TO RUN

Addis Ababa is high and hilly, which makes it an excellent place for ambitious runners to train. The sport is very popular and the city has produced some world-class athletes.

Every November the city hosts the Great Ethiopian Run, the biggest road race in Africa. Around 37,000 competitors complete the course in a blaze of coloured shirts. The giant street party loops 10km (6mi) around the city.

MEGA MARKET

The Merkato in Addis Ababa is believed to be the biggest market in Africa, but it isn't an easy place to measure! Around 13,000 people work in a labyrinth of stalls that twists and turns in every direction. Shoppers flock here to buy coffee beans and other locally grown food.

KINGS, QUEENS AND CREEPY CRYPTS

Until 1974, Ethiopia had a monarchy that claimed to be directly descended from the kings and queens in the Bible. In Addis Ababa, the emperors occupied Menelik's Palace. A few blocks south you can still visit the Bete Maryam Mausoleum. To enter this underground burial place you have to climb down through a secret door hidden under a carpet.

ANCIENT AUNT LUCY

Addis Ababa's oldest and most famous resident is Lucy – an extinct species of primate who lived 3.2 million years ago. Since she was discovered in 1974, many have described her as the most important fossil ever found, because she shows how our humanoid ancestors moved from walking on all fours to standing upright. In Ethiopia, Lucy is called *Dinkinesh*, which means 'you are marvellous' in Amharic. Her bones are housed in the National Museum of Ethiopia.

TAKING THE RAP

Rhythms and songs are part of the fabric of Ethiopian life, but in Addis Ababa modern music like hip-hop is becoming increasingly popular. Many young artists are now rapping in Amharic, but some also rhyme in Ethiopia's other languages, such as Oromo and Tigrinya, as well as English. Their lyrics are often inspired by historical events, politics or local heroes – including the much-loved Ethiopian football team.

133

JERUSALEM

Despite being attacked many times and completely destroyed at least twice, Jerusalem has been around for 6,000 years. In 1538, Sultan Suleiman the Magnificent built the walls that still surround the Old City today.

CHURCH OF THE HOLY SEPULCHRE

Christians have made pilgrimages to this church since the fourth century. It is built on a site where many people believe Jesus was crucified, buried and resurrected.

WALLS OF JERUSALEM

Just over 4km (2.9mi) long and typically 12m (39ft) high and 2.5m (8ft) thick, the city walls have 34 watchtowers and 8 gates. It's still possible to roam around these fascinating ramparts.

THE WESTERN WALL

This ancient stretch of brickwork is even older than the buildings currently on Temple Mount. The Wall possibly dates as far back as 19 BC, to the reign of Herod the Great. It is a hugely important site in Judaism, and Jewish people visit regularly to pray and place prayer notes in the holes in between the stones. During *bar* and *bat Mitzvahs* (Jewish coming of age ceremonies) it can get really lively as families gather along the Wall to sing and dance.

NEW GATE

THE CHURCH OF THE HOLY SEPULCHRE

TOWER OF DAVID

HURVA SYNAGOGUE

THE WESTERN WALL

THE CITADEL

Also known as the Tower of David, the Citadel was originally a palace for Herod the Great. After he died the Romans moved in, but the tower has also housed Crusaders and Ottomans. Over the centuries it has been extensively rebuilt.

THE CHURCH
OF ST ANNE

THE DOME
OF THE ROCK

TEMPLE
MOUNT

AL-AQSA
MOSQUE

MOUNT OF OLIVES

As well as being the site of a 3,000-year-old Jewish cemetery, this tree-covered mountain ridge also features heavily in the Bible. The Mount of Olives is described as the place where Jesus ascended to heaven.

TEMPLE MOUNT

The most important site in Jerusalem's Old City, Temple Mount, has been used by Jews, Romans, Christians and Muslims for thousands of years. In Judaism it's the holiest place on the planet – the sacred spot where Adam was made and Solomon's Temple once stood. Jews face it when praying. For Muslims, the Mount is Islam's third holiest site.

THE DOME OF THE ROCK

This Islamic shrine with its giant gold rotunda is Jerusalem's most recognisable landmark. The Dome of the Rock has occupied the central spot on Temple Mount since 692, making it one of the region's oldest buildings.

AL-AQSA MOSQUE

After two earlier prayer houses were knocked down by earthquakes, Al-Aqsa mosque was built on Temple Mount in 1035. Crusaders used it as a palace when they captured Jerusalem in 1099, but it was restored when Saladin retook the city in 1187.

CITY OF DAVID

This amazing Bronze Age walled settlement is ancient even by Jerusalem's standards! The very oldest part of the city was excavated in the early 20th century. Some archeologists think that it could be the site of the palace of David – the boy who slayed Goliath before becoming a king of Israel. Jews also believe that David brought the Ark of the Covenant here 3,000 years ago. Local and visiting children enjoy wading along Hezekiah's Tunnel, a 500m (1,640ft) long passage of waist-deep water.

MEGA...
Masjid al...
900,000 w...
pilgrims ...
contains...

MEGA MALL

With 1,200 stores, the Dubai Mall is the world's biggest and busiest shopping mall. In 2014, 80 million people visited the colossal consumer cathedral, more than twice the number that flocked to major attractions such as New York's Times Square or Central Park. Within the belly of the mega mall is a whale-sized aquarium, where fish-spotters can peer at 33,000 marine animals (and the odd diver) swimming around in 10 million litres (2,199,692 gallons) of water.

CRANE CITY

At the height of the Dubai construction craze 30,000 cranes were operating in the city. That's a quarter of all the cranes on Earth!

DUBAI
UNITED ARAB EMIRATES Asia

When oil was discovered in Dubai in 1966, the city's fortunes were changed forever. It began to grow in both size and wealth at a staggering rate. An ultra-modern metropolis now stands in the sand in the United Arab Emirates, with loads of fancy shops and some of the most amazing and ambitious buildings on the planet.

TOMORROW THE WORLD! (MAYBE)

The city's most famous ongoing development is the 'World' – a series of artificial islands built in the shape of a world map in the waters of the Persian Gulf, 4km (2.5mi) off Dubai's coast. The idea was to sell each miniature country to the super-rich, but the plan hit a few bumps and only Greenland has been finished so far.

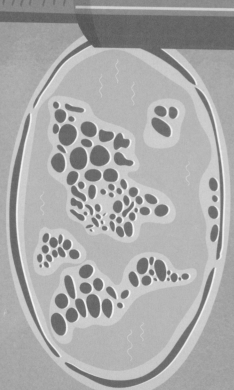

LIVING THE HIGH LIFE

Dubai's population of children hail from many different backgrounds. Only about one in ten of the people living in Dubai was born there. The local Emirati are typically wealthy. Families tend to live in modern, air-conditioned houses and, in the outskirts of the city. The apartments on the outskirts of the city. The and the kids go to private schools. The and the kids go to private schools. American and children of European, American and Australian ex-pats live in similar conditions and go to international schools.

BEHIND THE BUILDINGS

It takes years to build Dubai's manmade mountains, but who does all the heavy lifting? The city has a massive population of construction workers, mostly from Pakistan, Nepal, Bangladesh and India. Many labour in ferocious heat for low wages, and live in very basic conditions.

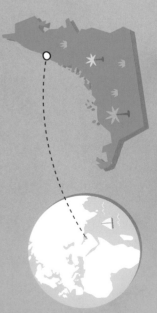

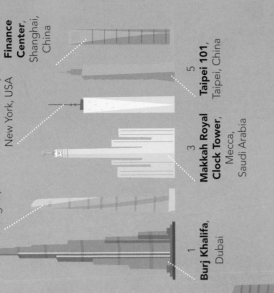

2
Shanghai Tower, Shanghai, China

4
One World Trade Center, New York, USA

6
Shanghai World Finance Center, Shanghai, China

3
Makkah Royal Clock Tower, Mecca, Saudi Arabia

5
Taipei 101, Taipei, China

1
Burj Khalifa, Dubai

DHOW AND THEN

The modern city is unrecognisable from the tiny traditional emirate that once perched on the banks of Dubai Creek, but it's possible to get a small taste of the old place by taking a creek cruise on a traditional *dhow* (Arabian boat).

PARK AND RIDES

In Dubai you can shoot through a shark tank in a waterslide and ski in an artificial snow centre complete with its own resident penguins – not bad for a city with an average temperature of 41°C (105°F)! Recently, Aquaventure and Ski Dubai have been joined by Legoland, a Bollywood-themed park and Motiongate, with rides inspired by Hollywood films, including *The Hunger Games.*

THE GIANT

The Burj Khalifa is the tallest building in the whole world, standing at a cloud-piercing 828m (2,716ft)! It will remain so until at least 2019, when the Kingdom Tower in Jeddah is due to complete its 1km (0.62mi) climb into the sky above Saudi Arabia. The Burj Khalifa is full of hotel rooms and private residences, but it's not necessarily easy living on the shoulder of a giant. It's so tall that the sun sets later for people on higher floors – all good, unless you're observing Ramadan, when Muslims are not allowed to eat until after sundown.

DID YOU KNOW...?

Burj Khalifa has **24,348** windows. It takes a crew of **36** workers up to four months to clean them all.

The building has **54** elevators, which can travel at **64kph (40mph).**

Don't even think about taking the stairs – the building has **163** floors.

SAMARKAND

UZBEKISTAN Asia

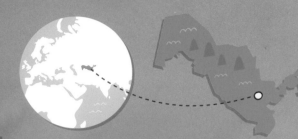

After invasions by Alexander the Great and Genghis Khan, 2,700-year-old Samarkand was transformed into a fairytale city by the legendary warlord, Timur (also known as Tamerlane). Today, Uzbekistan's most glorious and magical city boasts incredible squares, buildings and bazaars.

HORSING AROUND

Samarkand has a football team, FK Dinamo Samarqand, but a traditional sport called *Kupkari* is even more popular than soccer. Players on horseback attempt to pick up the headless body of a goat or calf and get it across a goal line. Up to 100 horses and riders can join in at one time, so play gets rough! Some participants wear old Russian army tank helmets and the riders' horse handling skills are legendary. Large tournaments are held at Samarkand's hippodrome.

BREAD WINNER

Siab Market is the beating heart of Samarkand – full of locals shopping, chatting, playing backgammon or watching street performers. The air all around is thick with spices. People munch on local specialities such as salted apricot pips roasted in ashes, while bakeries offer many kinds of golden Samarkand flatbread. The bread is baked in special ovens and is said to be unique to the city.

ROYAL STAR

Blackouts are a common annoyance for Samarkand's kids today, but the temporary lack of light pollution reveals the night sky as it was in 1424, when this was the astronomical capital of the world. Stargazing Prince Ulugh Beg – grandson of Timur – mapped an amazing 1,018 stars, creating a chart used by Greenwich Observatory, London, 250 years later. The remains of his ancient observatory can still be seen on one of Samarkand's hills.

LOVER'S LEAP

An old legend says that Samarkand, originally called *Marakanda*, was named after two tragic lovers – a beautiful princess called Kant (which means 'sugar' in the Uzbek language) and a poor boy called Samar, known for his bravery. When the king, Kant's father, discovered their forbidden love, he killed Samar. Kant was so heartbroken, she jumped from the roof of a castle.

COOL COSTUMES

Fabrics are also used to tell the city's history in El Merosi theatre. A historic fashion show presents costumes from different eras in Samarkand's past, from Scythian horsemen and warriors of the first millennium BC up to now.

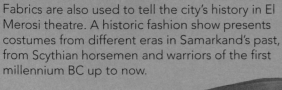

FOLLOW THE THREAD

The Silk Road (an ancient trade route between China and the Mediterranean) made Samarkand famous, and silk remains important to the city. Local women weave it into valuable carpets, which can take years to create. Every carpet contains a story, and some of the patterns have been around since Silk Road days.

MAGIC MOSAICS

Timur had an awful reputation for violence, but he never killed the artisans or architects in the places he conquered. Instead he sent them to Samarkand to sculpt his capital into a giant work of art. Samarkand became world famous in the 14th and 15th centuries as a place of beauty, because of the intricate mosaics around the Registan, Bibi-Khanym Mosque and the Shakh-I-Zinda cemetery. Now it's being carefully restored, tile by tile.

155

MUMBAI

INDIA Asia

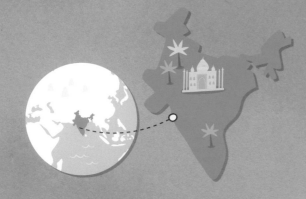

The mega-city of Mumbai, formerly known as Bombay, is home to 21 million people. It is one of the most densely populated urban areas on the planet. Life is hot and there isn't much wriggle room on the school bus, but Mumbai is also India's richest metropolis – a financial powerhouse that teems with workers and businesses.

LIFE'S SWEET

Mumbai is one of the best places to sample *mithai* (traditional sweets) from around the country and region. Delicious *Barfi* tastes like very sweet fudge, while buttery *Mysore pak* has the subtle taste of cardamom.

FAST FOOD

Mumbai has an army of 5,000 *dabbawalas* – food couriers who whizz around with carts delivering home-cooked lunches. Over 200,000 are dropped off at offices every single day. Although many *dabbawalas* can't read or write, it's estimated that they only make a mistake once per every eight million meals delivered.

TRAIN SPOTTING

Chhatrapati Shivaji Terminus (CST) is Mumbai's UNESCO World Heritage-listed train station. The building features dog-faced gargoyles on the outside, and there's usually some grimacing going on inside too, because this is the world's busiest railway station. Its 18 platforms allow around 1,500 trains to depart and arrive each day. During rush hour, up to 14 people squish into each square metre of the train, and it's common to see many hanging from the sides of the carriages.

CHHATRAPATI SHIVAJI TERMINUS

BEACH RITUALS

The famous sands of Chowpatty beach stretch down to the Arabian Sea. It's a crowded jumble of families, fortune-tellers, food vendors, snake charmers and dancing monkeys all jostling for space. In September the beach hosts massive Ganesh Chaturthi celebrations. Thousands of people flock from around the city to dunk icons of the elephant-head god into the sea.

THREE-FACED GOD

Elephanta is a short boat ride from the Gateway of India at Mumbai Harbour. The island boasts an amazing cave temple, hand-carved into the rock over 1,300 years ago. The main temple is dedicated to Lord Shiva, a Hindu god. Shiva is a complicated god with three faces who can be both kindly and fierce. He is shown in all forms in the cave – as creator, preserver and destroyer. The island's monkeys are similarly hard to read. One minute they look cute, the next they're trying to steal your snacks!

WELCOME TO BOLLYWOOD!

Mumbai is the epicentre of India's famous Hindi film industry, producing over 1,000 movies per year – more than twice as many as Hollywood. The brilliantly over-the-top films are typically colourful three-hour long extravaganzas. They feature an entertaining mix of comedy, drama, romance and – most importantly – music and dancing. In Mumbai you can take Bollywood tours and even try and get an on-screen role as an extra!

153

VARANASI

INDIA Asia

Varanasi is India's oldest city and the holiest place in the Hindu faith, clustered around the River Ganges. Hindus believe that we can be born again, and to die or be cremated here is seen as a great blessing. Death is all around, yet Varanasi is also full of life. Rickshaws race, temples glitter and children play in the streets.

GHATS TO THE GANGES

Varanasi is all about the sacred River Ganges and its *ghats* (steps leading into the water). This is where the faithful come to bathe, pray, perform rituals and say farewell to their dead. As soon as the first glow of sunrise settles on the water, people start arriving along the riverbank. Some practise yoga, others do their washing, sell trinkets or simply settle down to watch the day go by.

HARISHCHANDRA GHAT

This is one of two cremation *ghats*. For Hindus, cremation (the burning of a body) is an important tradition, and Varanasi is the holiest place to do it.

DASHASHWAMEDH GHAT

The city's most colourful and vibrant *ghat*, packed with flower sellers and crowds. Priests perform a dramatic ceremony every night at Dashashwamedh, with lots of fire and dancing.

MONKEY TEMPLE

Unsurprisingly, India's holiest city has temples everywhere. The bright red Durga Temple is one of the most important. It is also known as the 'Monkey Temple' because there are so many monkeys clambering over its walls.

ASSI GHAT

Around 300 pilgrims an hour arrive at the place where the River Assi meets the Ganges, but during festivals this can swell to an incredible 2,500. The visitors bathe and pay homage to an image of the Hindu god, Shiva. In the evening street sellers and entertainers come out, creating a party atmosphere.

DURGA TEMPLE

DASHASHWAMEDH GHAT

HARISHCHANDRA GHAT

RIVER

ASSI GHAT

FLOWER POWER

Pilgrims and visitors to Varanasi make fire and flower offerings to the Goddess Ganga, with an *aarti* – a small *diya* (candle and oil lamp), surrounded by blossoms, leaves and flowers – which is set alight and floated down the river.

MANIKARNIKA GHAT

Varanasi's most prestigious cremation *ghat* has a well, said to have been created when Parvati, the Hindu goddess of love, dropped her earring. Lord Shiva dug down to recover it, filling the hole with his sweat. *Manikarnika* means 'earring' in Sanskrit.

PANCHGANGA GHAT

A bathing *ghat*, built at the ancient meeting point of five streams. Women take sacred baths in the mornings on these steps during the months of *Vaisakha* (April and May) and *Karttika* (October and November).

SCINDHIA GHAT

This amazing Shiva temple is so ornate and heavy it lies partially submerged in the river. Many believe that Agni, the god of fire, was born nearby.

GAI GHAT

At Gai, a colourful statue of Shiva's sacred bull overlooks the Ganges.

MANIKARNIKA GHAT

PANCHGANGA GHAT

GAI GHAT

SCINDHIA GHAT

TRILOCHAN GHAT

GANGES

TRILOCHAN GHAT

Two turrets emerge from the river here – the water between them is considered especially holy.

BLESSED BRAHMINS

India has a caste system. At the top of society are the *Brahmins* (priests). They are the guardians of the Hindu faith, beginning their training when they are children. Only *Brahmins* can perform sacred rituals in the Ganges. The 'untouchables', or outcastes, are the very lowest members of society. They handle the bodies of people being cremated at the two burning *ghats*, carrying them through the alleyways of the old town.

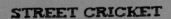

STREET CRICKET

The old town is a maze of *galis* – dusty, noisy and sometimes smelly alleyways where bulls wander aimlessly up and down. No one gets in their way because the animals are believed to be sacred. Instead local kids dodge their dung while playing cricket, the other religion in Varanasi.

THIMPHU

BHUTAN Asia

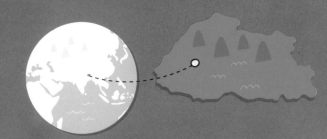

Perched like an eagle's nest high up on the southern slopes of the Himalayas, Thimphu is the capital of the kingdom of Bhutan. It's a totally unique place, watched over by a gigantic golden statue of Buddha himself. Thimphu echoes to chants from hilltop monasteries, flutters with colourful prayer flags and marks time with its own calendar.

CARE TO DANCE?

On the tenth day of the eighth month (by the Bhutanese calendar), the cloud capital holds a three-day festival – the Thimphu Tshechu. The streets of Thimphu overflow with colour and celebration, as thousands of people arrive in the city to join the festivities. Thimphu's monks are normally busy with silent prayer and meditation, but during this time they also join in the dance. *Atsaras* (Bhutanese clowns) caper and jest around the dancers, keeping away evil spirits.

GROSS NATIONAL HAPPINESS

Most countries measure their success by a scale called GNP (Gross National Product). GNP compares the amount of wealth that a nation's factories, farms and other industries produce. Bhutan measures its success on a unique scale – Gross National Happiness! It means that it's the happiness of Thimphu's people, not how much money or how many things they make, that is the measure of the city's success. Even the road signs promote happiness, reminding drivers to 'Let Nature be Your Guide' or that 'Life is a Journey. Complete it!'

BUDDHAS BY THE THOUSAND

Way back in the 8th century, a prophecy said that a giant Buddha would be built in the Thimphu hills. Now the people of this city are making those words come true. An amazing 51.5m (169ft) high statue of Buddha gazes over Kuenselphodrang nature park. The Buddha Dordenma is cast in bronze and covered in gold. The outside is finished, but inside 125,000 miniature Buddhas are still being constructed.

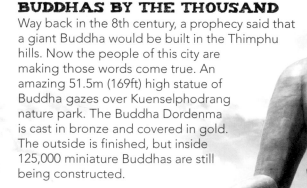

CLOUD CITY

Imagine living in a city nestled in the world's greatest mountain range. At 2,300m (7,500ft) above sea level, Thimphu is the third-highest capital in the world. Even so, this lofty city-in-the-clouds is dwarfed by the mighty peaks elsewhere in Bhutan. Some of the Himalayan giants soar to over 7,000m (23,000ft) above sea level.

MOTITHANG TAKIN PRESERVE

Ever heard of a 'cattle chamois'? Or a 'gnu goat'? These weird names both belong to a species of goat-antelope found only in the eastern Himalayas. The creature is properly known as a takin. The national animal of Bhutan is a docile creature that would happily spend all day eating grass and climbing mountains. When the King liberated all the takins from Thimphu's mini-zoo, they decided that they were happy to simply stay put. Respecting the animals' preferences, Thimphu set the area aside as the world's first (and only) takin reserve.

MOUNTAIN MONASTERIES

The Buddhist monasteries in Thimphu are places of great beauty. Tashichhoedzong is a massive structure in the heart of the city that also doubles as a fortress. No fewer than 30 temples and chapels are contained within its huge stone walls. Chagri Dorjeden was built out of stone and wood in 1620. This monastery clings to a rock face so high above the Thimphu Valley, it takes monks an hour to climb up to it from the road below.

SATURDAY 20 APRIL

SATURDAY 20 APRIL

THIMPHU TIME

Thimphu runs on its own time. It follows the Bhutanese calendar, a variation of the Tibetan calendar. Thimphu's people use it alongside their regular calendars.

ULAANBAATAR
MONGOLIA Asia

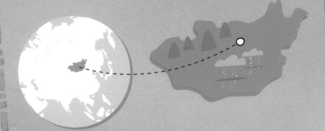

Between the wild, desolate grasslands of the Mongolian steppe and the vast, rugged expanse of the Khentii mountains, lies Ulaanbaatar. This vibrant city is a throbbing pulse in a surrounding wilderness. It's a cold, colourful place where Mohican-wearing punks mingle with Buddhist monks and suited professionals share the streets with visiting nomads.

STUFFED STATUE

Under communism, most of Mongolia's Buddhist buildings were destroyed, but Ulaanbaatar's Gandan Khiid monastery somehow managed to survive. Migjid Janraisig Süm is inside – a massive statue originally built for Bogd Khan (Mongolia's last king) when he was sick. It contains 27 tonnes (29.7 US tons) of medicinal herbs, 334 scriptures, 2 million bundles of mantras and an entire yurt complete with furniture. Bogd Khan also had a winter palace, which is now a museum. It boasts a pair of golden boots, a robe made from 80 foxes and a yurt lined with the skins of 150 snow leopards.

THE WARRIOR KHAN

There's no escaping Genghis Khan in Ulaanbaatar. The empire-building warlord conquered half the known world in the 13th century. He claimed almost 31 million sq km (12 million sq mi) of territory, more than any other leader in history. Khan caused the deaths of up to 40 million people in the process, but to Mongolians, he is a national hero. The warrior was born close to the capital and probably buried nearby, too. He brought the Silk Road under control and modernised the country – the city commemorates him in return with Genghis Khan Square.

MONGOLIAN MASH-UP

Ulaanbaatar isn't just about traditional music – modern styles like pop, rock and hip-hop are massively popular, too. Some bands have even started playing Mongolian instruments such as the horsehead fiddle alongside electric guitars and drums to create their own new sound.

TWIST AND SHAKE

Traditional dancing takes place in Ulaanbaatar's theatres. Men perform fast and fancy leg-kicks and somersault-style stunts, while super-flexible women fold themselves into truly eye-watering shapes. The dances are accompanied by traditional Mongolian throat singing and music played on strange and wonderful local instruments. The *morin khuur* is one of the most important. It looks like a viola, but has a scroll shaped like a horse's head.

Shagaa, a popular game in Ulaanbaatar, involves flicking sheep anklebones at a target.

FUN AND GAMES

The three so-called 'manly games' of Mongolia – archery, horse racing and wrestling – are celebrated at the huge Naadam festival every July. Nowadays women compete in archery and girls can participate in horse racing, too. Children start wrestling from as young as four, but many boys in the city prefer to take up more modern pursuits. Boxing and judo exploded in popularity after bringing Mongolia its first ever Olympic gold medals in 2008. Boxing, once banned under communism, is one of the country's fastest-growing sports.

LIFE IN THE FREEZER

Ulaanbaatar is officially the world's coldest capital, with an average January temperature of -33°C (-27.5°F). Kids wear lots of woolly layers, and everyone sips warming *suutei tsai*, salty milk tea. Despite the chill, many people in this fast-growing city still live in traditional Mongolian felt yurts called *gers*.

BĚIJĪNG

CHINA Asia

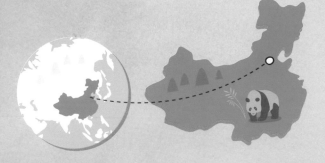

Běijīng bounces to the beat of 21 million people, working and playing under a sometimes smoggy sky. Reminders of the mega-city's extraordinary history are everywhere, but so are signs that Běijīng is looking ahead, too. Futuristic buildings and plans are already in place for when the city hosts the Winter Olympics in 2022.

WONDER WALL

Sadly it's not true that astronauts can see the Great Wall of China from outer space, but the ancient structure is truly colossal. Built by six ruling dynasties, the 2,300-year-old wall was originally 21,196km (13,170mi) long. What remains is mostly the 8,850km (5,500mi) Ming Dynasty Wall. The majority of the parts that can still be explored are clustered around Běijīng, including the most popular stretch, 80km (50mi) northwest of the city at Bādálǐng.

SO SQUARE

Tiān'ānmén Square sprawls across a brain-boggling 440,000 sq m (4,700,000 sq ft). That's the size of 352 Olympic swimming pools! Despite being the world's biggest public square, there is nowhere to sit down. The site contains the burial chamber of communist revolutionary Mao Zedong. After previous protests the area is now strictly patrolled by police, who zoom around on Segways. Every morning during the flag-raising ceremony, Chinese soldiers march through the Gate of Heavenly Peace and cross the square. Each soldier takes exactly 108 paces per minute, in strides that are 75cm (29.5in) long.

EMPERORS' PLAYGROUND

The Summer Palace was once an exquisite outside complex reserved for emperors of the Jin dynasty, but it's now open for everyone to enjoy. Three-quarters of the grounds are covered by wonderful water features. The palace is also home to a menagerie of bronze animals, including the mythical fire-breathing, hoofed and horned qílín.

PEKING MAN

The fossilized skulls and bones of very early human beings were discovered in a cave system in Běijīng in 1927. The Peking Man bones are believed to be 750,000 years old. During World War Two when Japan invaded China, the Chinese asked the USA to take the fossils out of China to protect them. The bones were last seen in December 1941 when they were packed into boxes to be handed over to US Marines. What happened next remains one of the greatest archeological mysteries of all time. The bones have never been seen again.

BIG BIRD'S NEST

The city's national stadium was unveiled for the Běijīng Olympics in 2008, soon earning itself the nickname of 'The Bird's Nest'. The woven design was inspired by the idea of a single thread wrapped round a ball. The stadium was built like this to make the structure earthquake-proof.

UGLY DUMPLINGS

Deep-fried scorpion anyone? How about a seahorse on a stick? Wángfǔjǐng Snack Street and night market in Běijīng's Dōngchéng district is the place to come if you have an adventurous stomach! There's everything here from multi-coloured *jiǎozi* (boiled dumplings) to sizzled snake, fried starfish and braised chicken feet. Local sweets are offered too, such as *tánghúlu* (candy covered fruits on bamboo sticks).

KUNG FU KIDS

Lots of traditional forms of fighting were born in China, including kung fu. Collectively these are known as *wǔshù*, which means 'martial arts'. *Wǔshù* is very popular in Běijīng, with boys and girls learning it from a young age. There are many academies operating in the city and tournaments happen all the time. Some feature full-contact fighting whilst others are displays using swords and other weapons.

PAGODAS AND PARKS

There are almost as many people in Běijīng as there are in all of Australia, but it's still possible to escape the crowds. The city has plenty of parks and green spaces, such as Beihai Park and the Back Lakes. These pagoda-studded playgrounds feature tranquil gardens and ancient buildings – including the Ming-dynasty Five-Dragon Pavilions.

BĚIJĪNG

The Ming dynasty didn't just make nice vases and build great walls, they also dreamt up the Forbidden City. The incredible complex in Běijīng served as the Chinese imperial palace from 1416 to 1911. Nearly a thousand buildings are spread across 72 hectares (178 acres). Today the Forbidden City is a UNESCO World Heritage Site.

FORBIDDEN PALACE

The biggest palace on the planet is surrounded by a 52m (170ft) wide protective moat. It was totally off-limits to ordinary people for years, just like Willy Wonka's fabled chocolate factory. For five centuries the emperors and empresses of the Ming and Qing dynasties went about their royal rituals behind firmly closed doors. Anyone caught trying to get in would be executed. Luckily visitors today can take a guided tour without any fear of punishment!

RULE BY NUMBERS

Numbers are very important in Chinese culture, and many details in the design of the Forbidden City were calculated precisely to accommodate this. For example, nine is considered a strong number and nine times nine is especially powerful. If you count the studs on the imperial doors in the Forbidden City you will find that they each have 81.

Qing dynasty emperors were carried around the palace on sedan chairs – all except the last one, Puyi, who pedalled around on a bicycle.

KOWTOW TO THE DRAGON

There is a colossal courtyard inside the Forbidden City that once held 100,000 people at a time (more than the Běijīng National Stadium's capacity), and three great halls. The 15th century Hall of Supreme Harmony is the most important because it's where all the big royal coronations and parties took place. When the emperor was sat on the Dragon Throne here, the whole court had to touch the floor nine times with their foreheads. This was known as *kowtowing*. In the Imperial gardens, there are two bronze elephants with front knees that bend the wrong way. They show that even elephants had to *kowtow* to the emperors.

PURPLE POWER

Now known by most locals as the Palace Museum or *Gù Gōng* (ancient palace), the older name, Zǐjinchéng, translates poetically as 'Purple Forbidden City'. The purple part (*Zǐ*) refers to *Zǐwēi* (the North Star), where, according to Chinese astrology, the Celestial Emperor had his palace. The Forbidden City was the equivalent home on Earth. *Jìn* means 'Forbidden'.

WOOD YOU BELIEVE IT?

The Forbidden City boasts 980 buildings. All of them are ancient and most are made of wood – in fact, the city officially houses the largest collection of preserved ancient wooden structures in the world. Some are built from incredibly precious Phoebe zhennan wood. This type of timber was so expensive only royalty could afford to use it. Even today zhennan can cost over £6,500 per cubic metre (35.3 cubic feet). Other materials used include marble and golden bricks.

PAINTING THE TILES... YELLOW

If you were a Chinese emperor, your favourite colour had to be yellow. As this was the tradition, almost every roof in the Forbidden City once had yellow tiles.

CHÉNGDŪ
CHINA Asia

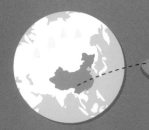

Chéngdū nestles in the heart of a legendary land of abundance, but few outsiders know much about it. The capital of China's Sìchuān region seems happy to keep a low profile. Indeed, up until a few years ago even the locals didn't realise that they were living right beside a long-lost kingdom. Chéngdū is an intriguing blend of laidback teahouses, spicy restaurants, noodles and gorgeous giant pandas.

SUPER POOL

On weekends, fun lovers from Chéngdū travel to Dàyīng Dead Sea resort, 130km (80mi) away. The new leisure palace is centred around a gigantic swimming pool. The splash zone is so vast, up to 10,000 people can float around at the same time! The pool has 400m (1,312ft) of 'coastline', a huge fake beach and its own seaside village.

TALES OF THE RIVERBANK

Wangjiang Park hugs Jǐn River as it passes through the city. Kids love to get out in little boats here and explore the pretty banks and glades. Over 100 varieties of bamboo grow in this great green park full of pagodas and pavilions.

TEA TIME

Chéngdū has a long tradition of growing tea and a reputation for having the best teahouses in all of China. These venues are usually full of locals playing a tile game like mahjong or Chinese chess *(xiàngqí)*. The aim is to relax as you sip. Many customers in the 6,000 Chéngdū teahouses enjoy chair massages or a more traditional Chinese treatment such as an ear cleaning!

RED HOT CHILLI PEPPERS

As the capital of Sìchuān, an area world-famous for its hot chillies and numbing peppercorns, Chéngdū likes to keep its menus spicy! Hotpots and sweet water noodles are local favourites, but you can also try something a bit more adventurous, such as *shuǐzhǔ yú* (carp or catfish served in chilli oil), or *fūqī fèipiàn*, which translates as 'married couple's offal/lung slices'. *Fūqī fèipiàn* combines shavings of chilled beef tongue or heart, with thin slices of tendon and tripe. Yum!

PANDA PUPS

The mountains around Sìchuān are home to China's most famous animal resident – the giant panda. Everyone loves these big black-eyed animals, but unfortunately habitat destruction has put the bears on the endangered species list. Chéngdū's Giant Panda Breeding Research Base tries to put this right, offering shelter to 120 giant and 76 red pandas. People are welcome to come and visit, but the base's real mission is to encourage the shy creatures to produce baby bears to release back into the wild. A recent success saw two pandas; Jing Jing and Si Yuan, give birth to two sets of male twins.

A giant panda needs to eat between 9 and 14kg (20-30lb) of bamboo shoots every day.

TURTLE CITY

Chéngdū is almost 2,000 years old and once boasted two city walls. According to legend, when the city was built in 310 AD, the architect followed the route of a turtle, letting the animal decide where the city's borders should be.

LOST KINGDOM

In 2001, during building work just outside the city centre, an astonishing set of 3,000-year-old ruins were unearthed. They turned out to be the remains of the old capital of the Shu Kingdom, an ancient civilization that lived along the Yangtze River. The Jinsha site has yielded all sorts of treasures. The Golden Sun Bird is one of the most spectacular – an almost pure gold disc featuring a 12-pointed sun and four flying birds.

HONG KONG
CHINA Asia

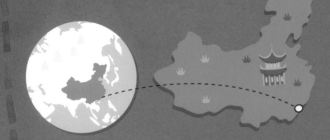

Hong Kong is one of the richest cities in the world – a forest of skyscrapers rising up from a few small islands off the south coast of China. The streets are a heady mix of ancient culture and neon lights. Hong Kong is just the place to catch a kung fu flick, go shopping in a 'mansion' house or nibble an extraordinary local dish. Mmm!

EVERYTHING EXCEPT THE TABLE

Hong Kong is famous for its food. There's a saying in China, that the Cantonese (the Chinese from this part of the country), "will eat everything that swims except a submarine, everything that flies except an airplane, and everything with four legs except the table." What would you say to a plate of thousand-year-old eggs (duck eggs kept in salt until they go black), baby mice in seaweed or monkeys' brains?

MONEY, MONEY, MONEY

There's cash in Hong Kong and lots of it. The city is one of the busiest trading centres in the world, right up there beside London and New York. It even has two skyscrapers, including one 484m (1,588ft) giant that's the sixth tallest building in the world. They were built just for the moneymen and women – the tallest one is called the International Commerce Centre.

SOAR IN A SEAPLANE?

Visitors flying into Hong Kong feel like they're about to land in the sea. That's because the airport takes over the whole of the tiny island of Chek Lap Kok, with extra runways built on land reclaimed from the ocean. It's perfectly safe, but many struggle to believe that as their plane swoops down over the water!

HOLLYWOOD IN THE EAST

Hong Kong has one of the biggest film industries in the world. Its kung fu action flicks, comedies and historical dramas have made big stars of actors and directors such as Jackie Chan, Wong Kar-wai and Maggie Cheung. A lot of the films made in Hong Kong star the city itself. The spectacular high-rises, steep green hills, twisting alleys, bright lights and dense crowds make the perfect backdrop.

TRAM-ENDOUS

Hong Kong locals love to travel by tram. On the northern part of the island clattering double-deckers known as 'ding dings' transport people to work or out to the shops. One of the best ways to see the city is to take the Peak Tram – one of the world's steepest funicular railways. The iconic cars make their way from the Garden Road Lower Terminus up the highest mountain on Hong Kong Island to the upper levels of the city. At the summit of the Peak there are beautiful houses, shops, restaurants and spectacular views.

HIGH-TECH...

There are more skyscrapers in Hong Kong than anywhere else on Earth. After dark the streets blaze with neon light. During the day, air-conditioned suspended walkways criss-cross the city to shield pedestrians from the scorching heat.

...AND TRADITION

Despite all of its state-of-the-art buildings, Hong Kong hasn't forgotten its traditions and customs. Construction workers helping to build the skyline clamber precariously up scaffolding made entirely of bamboo. Red-sailed junk boats bob in the harbour and in August people leave food out on the street and burn paper to appease the ghosts of their ancestors.

BANGKOK
THAILAND Asia

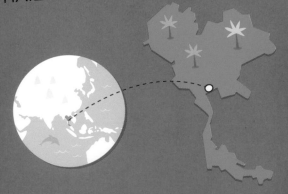

Bangkok is one of the hottest, busiest, hungriest and most thrilling places on Earth. From curving railways in the sky, revving *tuktuks* and crowded canals – this is a city on the go, all day, every day. Yet despite the unavoidable noise and pollution, Thailand's capital spills over with life, light and smiles.

TEMPLES BY THE THOUSAND

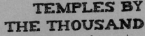

Bangkok is a city of temples, known as *wats*. The stunning Buddhist structures often feature multiple spires (*prang*), sweeping roofs, gleaming tiles and gold that glitters in the hazy tropical sun. The *wats* are both home and place of worship to Bangkok's thousands of orange-robed Buddhist monks, who spend much of their day in prayer. Two of the oldest and most magnificent temples are *Wat Phra Kaew* (Temple of the Emerald Buddha) and *Wat Arun* (Temple of Dawn).

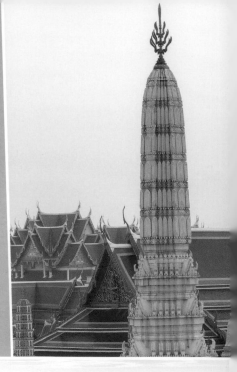

THAILAND'S ROYAL CITY

The Thai people adore their king. Pictures of his majesty Bhumibol Adulyadej are displayed all over Bangkok and a musical tribute is played in cinemas before every film. It's against the law to say or do anything insulting to Thailand's beloved monarch, who's ruled since 1946. When the King is in the capital, he lives in Chitralada Royal Villa, a moated palace huge enough to contain its own dairy farm.

HOT, HOT, HOT!
Bangkok might not have the world's greatest extremes of heat, but for round-the-clock, constantly sweaty temperatures it definitely wins the prize. The city sits about 1,500km (932mi) from the Equator, trapping heat between a concrete sprawl of buildings below and a thick cloud of pollution above. As a result it's almost always at least 30°C (86°F) in the city, day or night, all year round.

BANGKOK'S REAL NAME
You'll need to take a deep breath before you say Bangkok's full name. It's ...

KRUNG THEP MAHANAKHON AMON RATTANAKOSIN MAHINTHARA AYUTHAYA MAHADILOK PHOP NOPPHARAT RATCHATHANI BURIROM UDOMRATCHANIWET MAHASATHAN AMON PIMAN AWATAN SATHIT SAKKATHATTIYA WITSANUKAM PRASIT

IT MEANS:
'The city of angels, the great city, the residence of the Emerald Buddha, the impregnable city of Ayutthaya and the God Indra, the grand capital of the world adorned with nine precious gems, the happy city, abounding in an enormous Royal Palace that resembles the heavenly abode where reigns the reincarnated god, a city given by Indra and built by Vishnukarn.'

But don't worry. 'Bangkok' will do just fine.

THE GIANT SWING
Many visitors to Wat Suthat are surprised to see a giant red swing standing in its grounds. Towering at over 21m (68.9ft), the original swing was made in 1784 out of teak trees. In old Hindu ceremonies, young men used to climb onto the swing. They would fly higher and higher, trying to catch a bag of silver coins attached to a pole in their teeth. The ceremony was very dangerous and over time, several men fell to their deaths. Since 1932 the swing has been off-limits.

LIFE IN, ON AND ABOVE THE STREETS...
The first thing visitors notice about Bangkok are the crowds. In this city most of the action seems to take place outside on the streets. The sides of nearly every road are jammed with carts selling noodles, barbecued squid and other delicious food. Families socialise, neighbours go shopping and robed Buddhist priests come to collect supplies. The roads seethe with a constant river of trucks, *tuktuks* (motorbike taxis), cars, scooters and buses. The Thai government has even opened a railway high above the streets – the 36.4km (22.6mi) Skytrain.

...AND ON THE WATER
Bangkok's buzz doesn't stop at dry land – the Chao Praya (the 'River of Kings') flows through the heart of the city, feeding a network of canals that earned it the nickname 'The Venice of the East.' The canals are used for everything – washing, transport and even for floating markets, like Bang Khu Wiang, where farmers sell fruit, vegetables and chickens directly from their boats.

SINGAPORE

SINGAPORE Asia.

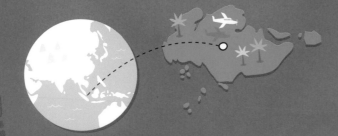

Singapore isn't just a city – it's a whole country! Alongside Monaco and the Vatican City, it's one of the world's few city-states. Despite its tiny size, Singapore is one of Asia's richest and most powerful centres. The ultra-modern metropolis is also a 'city in a garden', surrounded by lush green spaces, ancient rainforests and muddy wetlands.

A REAL MISHMASH

Singaporeans come from all over the world. You can hear the languages, see the festivals and enjoy the music from Malaysia, India, Europe and many other places. The largest group by far however, traces its ancestry back to China. Mandarin, the biggest language in multilingual China, is also Singapore's most widely spoken language.

TIME FOR A CHANGE

For such an organized city, Singapore seems to be a little confused about time. Since 1905, the city-state has changed its time zone a staggering six times! These have been prompted by events such as the Japanese invasion during World War Two, as well as time changes by its nearest neighbour, Malaysia.

WHAT'S A MERLION?

Singapore means 'Lion City'. In Malay (the language spoken in the Malaysian Peninsula and its islands), *singa* means 'lion', and *pura* means 'city'. It sounds very grand, but the reason for the name is a bit of a mystery. There have never been any lions in the area as far as anyone knows, and the city's official emblem is actually the 'merlion' – a half-fish, half-lion statue that spits water into Marina Bay.

SINGAPORE'S GREEN HEART

Singapore's reclaimed space isn't just used for skyscrapers and apartments. The Gardens by the Bay, a vast area of park and artificial forest designed to make the city a greener, happier place, is built entirely on land taken back from the sea. It's no ordinary park, either. The Cloud Forest is planted up with the kinds of jungle found on mountainsides in Southeast Asia and South America, while the Flower Dome recreates the environment of Mediterranean countries such as Greece and Spain. The Supertrees Grove cultivates ferns, vines and flowers on artificial trees that tower up to 50m (164ft) high. Best of all, there's a Children's Garden, complete with trampolines, balancing beams and rope bridges to clamber across!

LET THEM EAT CRAB

All that diversity means one thing for the people of Singapore – amazing things to eat! This is one of the world's greatest food cities. Locals go to enormous lengths to find the best chilli crab, fish-head curry or *sambal* stingray (stingray in a hot and spicy sauce).

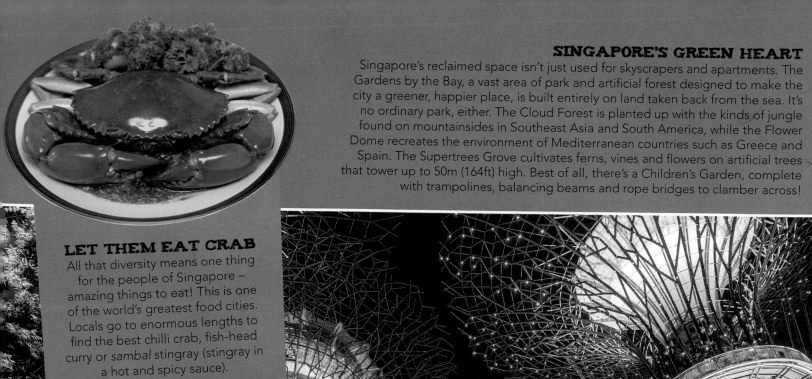

ANTI-ATLANTIS

Singapore is truly tiny, covering just 715 sq/km (276 sq/mi). Although space is tight, the population is high. Well over five million people call Singapore home and that number is rising rapidly. So what's the solution for this rich, resourceful city? Just make more land! Rather than sinking into the water, Singapore is rising above it. By 2030, the city plans to reclaim more than 56 sq/km (21.6 sq/mi) from the surrounding ocean.

NIGHT SAFARIS

Singapore has the world's first nocturnal zoo – the humid, open-air park only opens its gates after the sun goes down. Zoologists know that lots of animals prefer to come out after dark, so they decided to build a park that would allow people to watch them when they are at their most active. Visitors ride trams or take night-time walking trails to observe the animals in habitats just like their natural homes. Clouded leopards, flying foxes and spotted hyenas all lurk in the shadows.

☐ ORIGINAL ISLAND
■ NEW LAND

HANOI

VIETNAM Asia

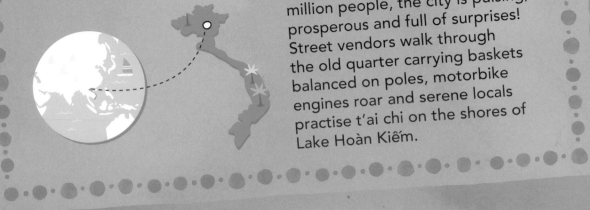

Steamy, hectic Hanoi is the capital of Vietnam. Home to over six million people, the city is pulsing, prosperous and full of surprises! Street vendors walk through the old quarter carrying baskets balanced on poles, motorbike engines roar and serene locals practise t'ai chi on the shores of Lake Hoàn Kiếm.

MAKE A HOG OF YOURSELF IN HANOI

Hanoians eat lots of rice, vegetables and noodles, so their food is super-fresh and super-healthy. *Bánh bao* are sweet, steamed buns with chicken, quail eggs and many other fillings, while *bún cha* is grilled pork with soup, noodles, green papaya and herbs! *Nước mắm* goes into almost every dish – a sauce made from small fish that have been salted and fermented. It tastes much better than it sounds!

TURTLES, SWORDS AND EMPERORS

The bright green lake, Hoàn Kiếm, sits in the very centre of Hanoi. It's a place of peace in the heart of a hectic city. According to legend, it was here that Lê Lợi, the Emperor who defeated the Chinese, returned his sword to the Golden Turtle God, Kim Qui. Until January 2016, a rare soft-shelled turtle called *Cụ Rùa* (Great Grandfather Turtle) could be seen swimming slowly across Hoàn Kiếm. He has sadly passed away, and it's thought that he was the only one of his kind.

SOARING DRAGON CITY

People have lived on the banks of the Red River for over 5,000 years. There have been so many kingdoms, cultures, invaders, religions and colonizers come and go during this time, it's almost impossible to keep up! Vietnam's capital was officially founded in 1010 AD by the Emperor Lý Thái Tô. He named the city *Thăng Long*, or 'Soaring Dragon'.

WALKING ON WATER?

It's hard to believe your eyes at Hanoi's Thăng Long puppet theatre – the brightly-coloured wooden puppets seem to dance, skip and run across the surface of a pond! The lacquered puppets, which can weigh up to 15kg (33lb), actually sit on big rods of bamboo. Skilful puppeteers pull their strings, staying hidden behind a painted screen. Water puppetry has been going on in Vietnam for nearly a thousand years – originally, the performances were held in flooded rice fields.

MOTORBIKES AND MAYHEM

Hundreds of thousands of cars, buses, trucks, pushbikes, horse-drawn carts and *cyclos* (bike taxis) choke Hanoi's streets, 24 hours a day. The most popular form of transport is the motorbike – the city has around four million. Swarms of bikes growl at every intersection, revving, teetering, blowing smoke and waiting to get going again. It's not unusual to see whole families piled up on a single bike, with adults at the front and kids hanging off on the back. The vehicles are also used to carry pigs, chickens and ducks, eggs, baskets and even TVs!

FRANCE IN THE TROPICS

People visiting Hanoi are often surprised by the number of French things they come across in the city – there are bakeries selling croissants and baguettes, cafés serving *café au lait* (milky coffee) and buildings that look like they've been plucked straight out of a Parisian street. This is all because Hanoi was once the capital of Indochina, a colony ruled by France from 1887 to 1954.

LONG BIEN BRIDGE

One of Hanoi's most famous sights is Long Bien Bridge, a 2.4km (1.49mi) structure that arches across the Red River. When it was first built, in 1902, it was one of the longest bridges in the world. Despite being repeatedly bombed by the Americans in the Vietnam War, Long Bien stayed up. Although it is a bit battered and rusty, it still connects Hanoi to the port of Haiphong.

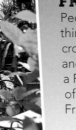

MANILA
PHILIPPINES Asia

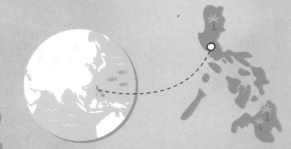

Manila is mammoth – a vast, sprawling metropolis that appears to never end. With its beautiful Spanish buildings, resourceful people and truly astonishing food, the city deserves its reputation as the 'Pearl of the Orient'. Underneath its glossy modern shell there is a treasure trove of life, colour and tradition.

A BIT SQUEEZY

The Metro Manila area is a massive urban sprawl radiating out of central Manila. This is a true megacity, home to 22 million and counting. The old core of central Manila has nearly 43,000 people living inside each square kilometre (0.39 sq mi), making it easily the most crowded place on the planet. There's no point moving to the suburbs for a bit of room, either. The next two most crowded cities, Pateros and Caloocan, are also in the Manila Metro Area!

BULLFIGHTING IN THE TROPICS

Many of the buildings in Intramuros, the oldest part of Manila, are decorated with statues of Spanish kings and queens. The Spanish made Manila the capital of their Philippine colony for over 300 years – even the word 'Philippine' comes from the Spanish monarch, Philip II. Manila Cathedral is the most famous building in the Intramuros. It was first built in 1581, but the effects of war and earthquakes have meant that it has had to be rebuilt seven times since. The square outside the cathedral was once used as a bull-fighting ring.

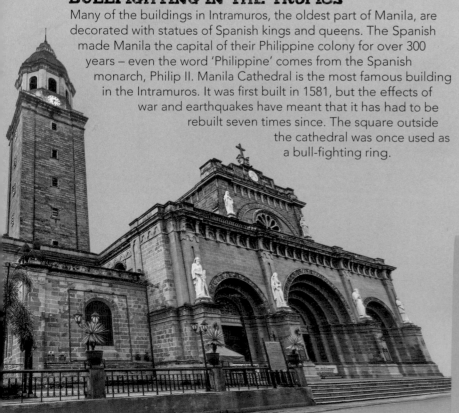

FAR-OUT FOODS

Newcomers need to be brave when they order from a typical Manila menu. Those who have grown up eating *balut* (a boiled duck egg with the unborn duckling cooked inside), *betamax* (cubes of solidified chicken blood, grilled over coals) or *sisig* (chopped pig's face and ears, mixed with chicken livers) know how scrumptious these things can be. Everyone else might need some time to adjust!

THE AMAZING PEOPLE OF PAYATAS

Manila is the capital of a country still trying to fight its way out of poverty. Nowhere is this fight more desperate than in the neighbourhood of Payatas. The community has become known for the Payatas Dumpsite, a massive open-air rubbish tip that's home to more than 80,000 residents. The millions of tons of garbage piled up on the site makes for a dangerous environment – fires often break out and in 1998 a landslide killed more than 200 people. Despite this, the dumpsite offers some refuge for people who have few other ways to keep themselves alive. The scavenger-citizens of Payatas are resourceful and highly organised, and even have their own football team.

WHATEVER YOU WANT, WE'VE GOT IT...

If you can't buy it in this city, you probably won't be able to buy it anywhere! Anything and everything is for sale – chicken heads, fake mobile phones, branded T-shirts and exotic fruit by the barrow-load. Divisoria Market in Chinatown is a huge, noisy, overwhelming maze of stalls. Nobody could visit them all, even if they shopped from breakfast to bedtime.

UNDERGROUND MANILA

Underneath Bonafacio Global City, a modern part of Manila that bristles with skyscrapers and businessmen, lies a huge network of tunnels. The 32 chambers were cut into the rock by Americans in 1910, and once ran under the military complex, Fort McKinley. The tunnels were later taken over by the Japanese when they captured Manila in 1942. They were returned, along with the fort, to the Filipino people when they gained their independence in 1946. The underground passageways are off-limits to the public, but the entrances are still hidden behind unmarked grates and doors all across this busy part of town.

175

TOKYO
JAPAN Asia

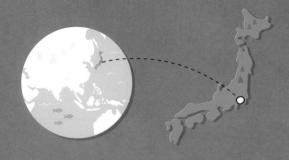

Tokyo is over the top. It's the biggest, fastest, flashiest city on Earth, and no one can ever say that they've seen it all. The metropolis wakes up early to the sound of fishermen touting their wares at the Tsukiji Market, buzzes all day to the whir of commuter trains, then whiles away the nights to the cheers of sumo wrestling fans and the beat of karaoke bars.

FISHY BUSINESS

One of Tokyo's great sights is the Tsukiji Fish Market. It's the biggest in the world, accounting for much of the 700,000 tonnes (771,600 US tons) of seafood that passes through the megacity every year. Tsukiji has become such an amazing spectacle, the market once had to ban tourists from the pre-dawn auction, where all the best fish (especially gigantic tunas) get snapped up. Some of the specimens fetch such enormous sums of money that students wanting to fund their gap year have been known to rent fishing boats and then bring in their best catches to sell.

CAN YOU HANDLE THE HEAT?

Tokyo's *onsens* (hot springs) are the ideal antidote to the crazy pace of city life. There is a lot of volcanic and geothermal activity all over Japan, creating thousands of mineral springs that are heated by the rocks below. For hundreds of years, Tokyo residents have loved relaxing in the natural baths, either with their work colleagues, friends or families. The minerals in the water are believed to be very nourishing. The locals head to the *onsens* to relieve all sorts of aches and pains.

TOKYO BY NUMBERS

Price of one night in the most expensive hotel	1 million yen (£6,364)
Number of vending machines	over 400,000
Cost of a meal at the most exclusive restaurant	50,000 yen (£269)
Days per year that Mount Fuji is visible from the city	79
Percentage of Japanese-born residents	97.5

SUPER-SIZE

Megacities have a population of at least 10 million people. In recent years, more and more of these monster metropolises have popped up around the world, but Tokyo remains the daddy of them all with over 37 million residents. The 'Greater Tokyo Area' stretches all the way to Yokohama – a former sleepy fishing village that has now become a major port city in its own right.

STUFF THE TRAIN!

Tokyo's metro system is mind-bogglingly complex. It's really three systems linked together, creating a network of over 300km (186mi) of track. The almost constant flow of trains transports in excess of 3.2 billion (yes, billion!) people per year. The rush hour on some of the lines gets so crowded that white-gloved oshiya or 'train-stuffers' are employed to push people on-board, packing as many as possible into each carriage.

SUMO CENTRAL

Japan is famous for its sumo wrestlers. Fans flock to Tokyo's Ryogoku Kokugikan (National Sumo Hall) to see their favourite sporting stars compete. Enormous wrestlers called *rikishi* try to force their opponents either to leave the ring or touch the ground with anything other than the soles of their feet. It might look simple, but *rikishi* have to begin their training when they're still children. Maintaining the ideal sumo weight of over 200kg (31st) isn't easy either. *Rikishi* have to eat one or two enormous meals per day, tucking away at least 10,000 calories. Sumo is a traditional sport that can trace its origins back to the national religion, Shintō.

177

TOKYO

High-tech Tokyo looks like a set from a science fiction film. In neighbourhoods like Shinjuku, Ginza and Harajuku, forests of neon run up each building, blazing with symbols, cartoon characters and numbers. When the sun comes up, Tokyo's youngsters add even more colour, strutting their stuff in cute and kooky outfits.

MARVELLOUS MACHINES

In a city that never sleeps people like to know that they can get what they need, whenever they need it. Luckily, there are plenty of vending machines to help them out 24/7. Tokyo is stuffed full of the mechanical boxes! There's almost nothing that shoppers can't find. Fresh eggs, rice, piping hot jacket potatoes and even lettuce are just the touch of a button away!

CAT CAFÉ

How do you chill out in the world's biggest and busiest city? Many Tokyo residents head to a cat café! As well as enjoying a snack or a drink, they pay to stroke and play with one of the cafés furry friends. It's often not possible for them to do this at home because many apartments don't allow residents to keep pets. Some cafés even offer sessions with rare cats and *manga* comic books for their customers to read.

LIVING IN A BOX

No building better sums up the fabulous, futuristic architecture of Tokyo than the Nakagin Capsule Tower. It was designed by architect Kisho Kurokawa as a place where people could both live and work. The building looks like a stack of washing machines piled on top of each other. Space inside each capsule is as limited as it looks. Each pod measures just 10 m² (108 sq ft) with a bathroom the size of an aeroplane toilet. Plans are underway to either demolish the tower or to keep the design and update it to meet modern needs. For now, it's still possible to rent a pod in this incredible structure.

SCRAMBLE IN SHIBUYA

The streets around the Hachiko Exit of Shibuya Station are some of the most dazzling in the city. At night, they're an awesome mix of flashing signs and giant video screens, pulsing with light and movement. The scene at ground level is equally stunning. Below the neon, thousands of people every minute stream across 'The Scramble' – the busiest pedestrian crossing in the world.

HARAJUKU

In the Harajuku district, everybody likes to stand out! Tokyo's teenagers gather to show off their over-the-top street fashion, competing with each other to come up with more and more outrageous costumes. There are huge platform shoes, bright pink tutus and crazy, multi-coloured hair extensions. Fans of 'cosplay' (short for costume and play) hang out together dressed up as their favourite action heroes and comic book villains. Every costume has to be perfect, right down to the masks, wings and laser-guns.

179

KYOTO
JAPAN Asia

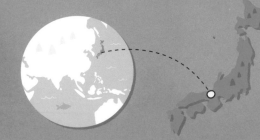

Japan's former imperial capital, Kyoto, perfectly showcases the nation's ancient traditions and architecture. Secret temples and shrines pepper the city and surrounding mountainsides, confectioners create sweets to reflect the blossoms that are in bloom and revered geisha women, with their powder white faces and painted red lips, bustle elegantly down the streets.

SAKURA SPOTTING
One of the most magical times in Kyoto is early spring when the beautiful pink *sakura* (cherry blossoms) burst out of the trees. The most famous *hanami* (cherry-blossom viewing) spots are Maruyama Park and the Heian Shrine. The blossom season only lasts for about two weeks, but people get so excited they put on *sakura*-patterned kimonos and party under the trees.

DAINTY DISHES
The Japanese take their food very seriously and Kyoto is definitely one of the best places to eat in the whole country. *Kaiseki* cuisine is the most famous, where chefs show off their skills by serving lots of tiny, beautifully presented dishes. Diners sitting down to a typical *kaiseki* meal would get up to 15 courses, probably including *mukozuke* (sashimi or raw fish), *konomono* (Japanese pickles) and *yakimono* (grilled fish).

GION GEIKA
Kyoto is the heart of Japan's geisha world. The neigbourhood of Gion, with its traditional wooden townhouses, teahouses and gardens, is home to the geisha (here known as *geiko*) women of Kyoto. Geisha are ladies who have trained for years in traditional Japanese arts to become the perfect entertainers. Girls begin training from the age of 15 as *maiko* (pronounced 'my-ko'), before gaining *geiko* status. They learn music, dance, tea ceremonies and conversation. With their coiffured hairstyles, lavish kimonos and distinctive *okobo* (wooden sandals) they resemble moving works of art.

A CITY OF TWO HALVES
When it comes to status, Tokyo is just a newcomer. Kyoto was the imperial capital of Japan for over a thousand years, between 794 and 1868. It was originally designed as a square-shaped city, neatly split into two halves – the 'Right Capital' and the 'Left Capital'. A central avenue divided the sectors, with the emperor's palace presiding at the top. This perfect shape (which is hard to see now that Kyoto is covered in modern buildings) was supposed to mirror the perfect order of the empire.

180

WET YOUR WHISTLE AT KIYŌMIZU

Kyoto is a very spiritual place – it has over 2,000 Buddhist temples and Shintō shrines. Shintō is an ancient Japanese religion, in which people worship gods called *kami*. Perhaps the most extraordinary temple is the Buddhist Kiyōmizu-dera Temple, perched on the side of Mount Otowa. There has been a shrine here for over 1,200 years. While the current buildings 'only' date back to the 17th century, they're among some of the most beautiful in the country. There's a waterfall in the centre of Kiyōmizu, from which visitors can drink the sacred water of Otowa.

MIGHTY NIJŌ CASTLE

Nijō Castle is one of Kyoto's greatest sights. It belongs to a time now known as the 'Warring States' period, when Japan was a violent and lawless country and warlords fought each other for power. Nijō Castle was built at the very end of this era, between 1601 and 1603. It became the Kyoto home of the Tokugawa Shogun (a military governor and head of the Tokugawa family). The castle boasts two sets of walls, a moat, multiple gates and the Ninomaru Gōten, a splendid palace built out of gold and precious wood.

NEVER BE RUDE TO A SAMURAI

During the Tokugawa period, the Shogun employed fierce warriors to defeat his enemies and control the people. These were the samurai, men who lived by a code called *bushido*. The samurai increasingly became rulers rather than warriors during the relatively peaceful times of the Tokugawa period, but they were still allowed to use their swords on any commoner who didn't show them enough respect! There are no samurai left today, but Kyoto has many sites – like the Sanjō Bridge – that are associated with the legendary swordsmen.

181

PYONGYANG

NORTH KOREA Asia

Pyongyang, ruled by the Workers' Party of Korea, is a fascinating and secretive city of monumental buildings and public festivals. Though it's existed since 1122 BC, its modern skyline was built from scratch after World War Two. Behind the pomp, the North Koreans go about their every day business – picnicking on Moran Hill, strolling by the Taedong River and playing volleyball in their lunch breaks.

THE STORY OF THE TWO KOREAS

Korea has been divided into two countries since the end of World War Two. After the separation, conflict developed between the north (backed by China and the former Soviet Union) and the south (backed by the United Nations, USA and other countries). The Korean War occurred between 1950 and 1953, and ended with nobody winning. The country was formally divided into the Democratic People's Republic of Korea in the north and the Republic of Korea in the south. A no man's land called the DMZ (Demilitarized Zone) still separates them.

THE FAMILY BUSINESS

North Korea has only ever had three 'Supreme Leaders' – Kim Il-sung (who died in 1994), his son Kim Jong-il (who died in 2011) and his grandson Kim Jong-un, who is in government now. The people of Pyongyang are devoted to their ruling family. Although Kim Il-sung died over 20 years ago, he is still recognized as North Korea's president. Kim Jong-un, the 'Great Successor', is the world's youngest state leader, although his exact date of birth remains a secret.

NO VACANCY (YET)

After being largely destroyed during the Korean War, Pyongyang was rebuilt from scratch to an elegant plan. These days the central city looks very grand – there are wide, straight streets, monumental buildings and lots of impressive statues. The pyramid-shaped Ryugyong Hotel is definitely the most eye-catching of all, towering over 330m (1,082ft) into the sky. It's hard to get a room there, however. Although construction started in 1987, it still hasn't opened for business!

KUMSUSAN PALACE OF THE SUN

Once a government building, then a palace for the leaders of North Korea, the fabulously named Kumsusan Palace of the Sun is now the world's largest mausoleum. When the first leader of the country, Kim Il-sung, died his son reportedly spent £67 million converting Kumsusan into a resting place for the Supreme Leader. Now both father and son lie there, embalmed and under glass, as admiring visitors are carried slowly past on a travelator.

SINGING IN THE REIGN

The people of Pyongyang love to sing and most bars have a karaoke machine. City dwellers like to croon along to popular western music including The Beatles and Celine Dion, but they also have their own girl band called Moranbong. It is said that the girls in the band were handpicked by Kim Jong-un! They each sing and play their own instruments.

PECKISH IN PYONGYANG?

People in Pyongyang like to eat lots of rice, noodles, pickles and vegetables, plus just a little meat. The one thing on offer in all of Pyongyang's few restaurants is *kimchi*. Usually made with cabbage, *kimchi* is a blend of vegetables fermented with chilli and salt. It's fiery, delicious and no table in the city ever does without it.

RUNGRADO 1ST OF MAY STADIUM

Pyongyang has the largest stadium in the world, built for the public celebrations the government likes to hold regularly. Named the Rungrado 1st of May Stadium, it seats an amazing 150,000 people, which is twice as many as Manchester United's Old Trafford. Rungrado is used for football, athletics and North Korea's gymnastic and artistic games, the Arirang Festival.

SEOUL
SOUTH KOREA Asia

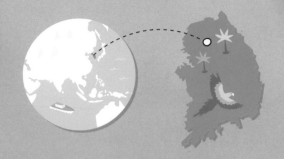

Seoul is one of Asia's success stories. Since becoming the capital of South Korea in the 1950s, its growth and wealth has skyrocketed. Life is sweet in this historic yet forward-facing city. Classic pagodas and teahouses mingle with shining towers, digital screens and bright neon signs. The capital certainly deserves its official name, 'Seoul Special City!'

EYES ON THE PRIZE

Seoul kids are brought up not to take life for granted. They are expected to work hard at school and take responsibility for their future. To make sure they make the grade many attend *Hagwon* or 'cram school' until midnight. Young Seoulites are also taught the value of money. Many are encouraged to save and soon learn to seek out a bargain, haggling with the city's street vendors.

A RIVER RUNS THROUGH IT... AGAIN

One of the most amazing displays of modern Seoul's wealth is the Chonggyecheon Stream. As the city grew, a creek running through the downtown area was concreted over and a motorway built through the middle. However in 2003, the authorities decided that the city was missing one of its most important natural features. The concrete was dug up and the motorway was moved. A stunning 11km (7mi) ribbon of clean water, parks and public space was carved through the middle of the city. The cost? A cool £260 million!

TECHNICOLOUR TAXIS

The streets of this busy capital rumble with the engine hum of hundreds of taxis. To make things easier, they use a special colour code. Deluxe taxis, which are safer and have better drivers, are black with a gold stripe, while ordinary cars are white and silver. Taxis for visitors who can't speak Korean are bright orange with the Seoul mascot – a fire-eating dog called Haechi – painted on the side.

CHANGDEOKGUNG PALACE

Built as one of five Grand Palaces by the Joseon Dynasty in the 14th century, Changdeokgung is a 44.5 hectare (110 acre) complex of royal halls, towering gates, libraries, private rooms and breathtakingly beautiful gardens. Unfortunately the palace has been burnt or badly damaged several times over the years. Every time, Changdeokgung has been reconstructed exactly to the original plan.

LOFTY LIVING

Nearly half of South Korea's population live within the Seoul Capital Area, the fifth largest metropolitan area in the world. There are more people based there than there are in the whole of Australia. The majority of Seoul's inhabitants live in massive high-rise apartment blocks. The Samsung Tower Palace looms 72 storeys into the sky, making it the tallest residential complex in Asia.

DONGDAEMUN DESIGN PLAZA

The Dongdaemun Design Plaza opened its doors in 2014. This futuristic structure is home to the latest in Korean and international design. It's got space for exhibitions and conferences, labs where engineers and inventors can work on their innovations and shops where visitors can buy the latest, beautifully designed gadgets.

WIRED WONDERLAND

South Korea is one of the most technologically advanced countries in the world and Seoul is certainly the most wired city on the planet. An astonishing 95 per cent of households have an Internet connection – even the subway has Wi-Fi! The city is dotted with digital display screens. Special Media Poles line the pavements, offering a place for pedestrians to look up information or snap a photo.

K-POP CULTURE

Pop fans in Seoul don't need to tap into the UK or US charts – South Korea has its own genre of music. K-pop (short for Korean pop) is full of colour, synchronized dance routines and bands with names like EXO and 2NE1. The artist Psy's track *Gangnam Style*, named after a district in the city, became the most watched video ever on YouTube.

DARWIN
AUSTRALIA Oceania

Sultry, remote and multicultural, Darwin is Australia's only tropical city. The outpost is closer to Asia than Sydney, giving it an atmosphere that is all its own. Nature is here in all its wild variety – whether it's the power of a swirling cyclone, the dramatic beauty of Darwin's national parks or the brooding menace of the saltwater crocodiles that hunt and hide in the harbour.

CALLING AUSTRALIA

Before telephones and the Internet came along, Darwin was a vital point in Australia's connection to the outside world. In 1872, the 3,200km (1,988mi) Overland Telegraph Line was laid from the south to the north. The line connected Adelaide to Darwin and then joined the new undersea cable to Java, Indonesia, allowing messages to be sent quickly between Australia and the rest of the world.

DARWIN

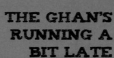

THE GHAN'S RUNNING A BIT LATE

One of the world's great trains, the Ghan, finishes its journey in Darwin. It runs nearly 3,000km (1,864mi) straight up the middle of the country. The train was first nicknamed the 'Afghan Express', in honour of the Afghani cameleers (camel handlers) who helped open up the parched deserts of inland Australia. Construction on the line first began in the 1880s, with plans to run all the way across the continent. It wasn't until over 120 years later, in 2004, that the line finally reached Darwin!

TERRIBLE TRACY

Darwin was unlucky enough to be the site of one of the worst natural disasters in Australian history – Cyclone Tracy. It was Christmas Day in 1974 when the city received the worst present imaginable. Furious winds of over 200 km/h (124 mi/h) flattened over 70 per cent of Darwin's buildings, killing 66 people. The Darwin standing today is almost completely new as the city had to be rebuilt from scratch.

LARRAKIA LAND

Darwin's oldest inhabitants, the Larrakia, have lived in and around the city for tens of thousands of years. They're also known as the 'Saltwater People' because they have such a close connection with the sea, beaches and mangroves that make up this lush land. Today the Larrakia are a bright, Aboriginal nation of around 2,000 people. They even have their own radio station – Radio Larrakia 94.5 FM.

Australia
Bombing of Darwin 1942
45c

ON THE FRONT LINE

Darwin is one of the few Australian cities to ever have come under attack. On 19 February 1942, while Japan was fighting against Australia in World War Two, it sent 188 fighters and bombers to attack Darwin, the major Allied base in northern Australia. During the course of two raids, 243 people were killed, 8 ships were sunk and 20 planes were destroyed.

ADELAIDE

LAZY TROPICAL DAYS

Darwin is a tropical paradise. It only has two seasons – the 'Wet' runs from November to April, while the 'Dry' stretches from May to October. The city rarely gets colder than 17°C (63°F) or hotter than 33°C (91°F). Its beaches and estuaries are fringed with green mangrove, palm, mango and frangipani trees. Inland there are wild, untouched national parks such as Kakadu and Litchfield. It's no wonder that Darwinians spend so much time outdoors!

SALTY CITY

The Northern Territory is home to over 100,000 saltwater crocodiles, the largest and most aggressive crocodile in the world. These ancient predators, which can grow up to 6m (19.7ft) in length, are quite at home in the mangroves and mudbanks of Darwin Harbour. The government tries to keep the crocs away from populated areas, but with the highest density of crocodiles anywhere in the world, there's always a few hanging around. A Darwin kite-surfer found this out to his cost in May 2015, only just managing to escape when a 2.5m (8.2ft) salty decided that it was feeling peckish!

PERTH

AUSTRALIA Oceania

Perth is sunny, easygoing and outdoorsy. There's space here and more to spare – the proud capital of Western Australia presides over a state so vast that much of Western Europe could fit inside! The Swan River runs through the heart of the city. Perthites gather there every day to swim, sail or throw some shrimp on the barbie.

SUN, SAND AND SURF

Perth is the sunniest capital on Earth, enjoying an average of eight hours per day. With all that warm weather and 19 beautiful beaches, it's not surprising that the surfies love the city and its coast. Trigg, Scarborough, Brighton and South Cottesloe are some of the top spots. Even the knowledge that they're sharing the water with one of the most perfectly designed predators in the natural world, the great white shark, doesn't turn these dedicated thrill-seekers away.

SAY CHEESE, QUOKKA!

From scuttling goannas to elegant brolga birds and playful dolphins, Perth is known for its amazing wildlife. The area is a biodiversity hotspot – teeming with flowers, plants and animals. With 71 types of reptile, the city is believed to have more species than any other urban area in the world. Recently however, it has become more famous for its lovable quokkas. Quokkas are small, furry marsupials that roam free on Rottnest Island. The little critters are so friendly, they have even sparked a selfie craze on Twitter.

LITTLE NIPPERS

After school and on the weekends, Junior Surf Lifesavers hit Perth's beaches. Local five to thirteen-year-olds, known as 'Nippers', dash in and out of the waves, learning how to swim, surf and save lives. Every life-saving club in the city has a junior Nippers programme. The children wear different coloured swim caps to show what age and stage they have reached.

THE BELLS, THE BELLS!

The banks of the Swan River seems like an unlikely spot to find some of the world's biggest musical instruments, but this is the home of the Swan Bells. The 18 massive bells hang in an 82.5m (271ft) tower called a campanile. The glass and copper tower was built to commemorate Australia's bicentenary, marking 200 years since the Europeans arrived in the country. When the Swan Bells are rung, their chimes can be heard for miles around.

TRIGG BEACH

SCARBOROUGH BEACH

BRIGHTON BEACH

ROTTNEST ISLAND

SOUTH COTTESLOE BEACH

SWAN BELLS

KINGS PARK

PERTH ZOO

SWAN RIVER

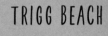

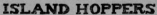

ISLAND HOPPERS

The Noongar people have been in Perth for a long time – tens of thousands of years, in fact. They can remember, through their songs and stories, when it was possible to walk on foot to the islands that lie offshore from the city. That was during the peak of the last Ice Age, a trifling 12,000 years ago. Today, the sandy islands of Rottnest, Garden and Carnac sit several kilometres off the coast of Western Australia.

MILES FROM EVERYWHERE

Perth is a wealthy oasis of beaches and parkland, perched in between the Indian Ocean and the desert. The locals like to say that they live in the most far-flung major city on Earth. In reality, that honour goes to Honolulu, the capital of Hawaii. Perth is a close second, however. It takes two days of non-stop driving to reach the eastern cities of Sydney and Melbourne, or four hours in a plane. With that much outback between them, perhaps it's no wonder that Perth is in a different time zone to the rest of Australia.

BALLARAT

AUSTRALIA Oceania

Ballarat, the state of Victoria's biggest inland town, might seem sleepy now, but back in the 1850s it was legendary! The city was at the centre of one of the biggest gold rushes the world has ever seen. Ballarat's fine Victorian buildings, neat botanical gardens and wide streets hint at the riches that once passed through the gold miners' hands.

1   GOLD!

Edward Hargraves, who'd been in California for the gold rush of 1849, was the first man to discover gold in Australia. As he walked through the bush near Bathurst in New South Wales, it suddenly occurred to him that the landscape looked a lot like California. Hargraves grabbed a spade, struck gold and changed history. Soon, gold was discovered further south, in Victoria. The Rush was on!

2   TENT CITY

News travelled slowly in the 1850s, but it was fast enough to send the magic 'gold' word all around the world. Hundreds of thousands of prospectors raced to Victoria. There were no houses available for the huge new populations that sprung up around the digging sites. When gold was found at Poverty Point in 1851, what had once been the sheep farm of 'Ballaarat' suddenly became, almost overnight, a tent city instead.

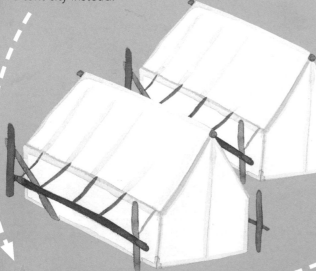

3   TROUBLE BREWING

Life was hard for most of the arrivals in the 'Golden City'. Few struck it rich. The surface gold quickly ran out and most had to sweat long days panning in rivers instead. Others dug deep shafts in the hope of finding a few nuggets buried in the earth. To make matters worse, the men were forced to buy expensive mining licences from the authorities. Soldiers would scour their diggings two or three times a week, arresting anyone without the right paperwork.

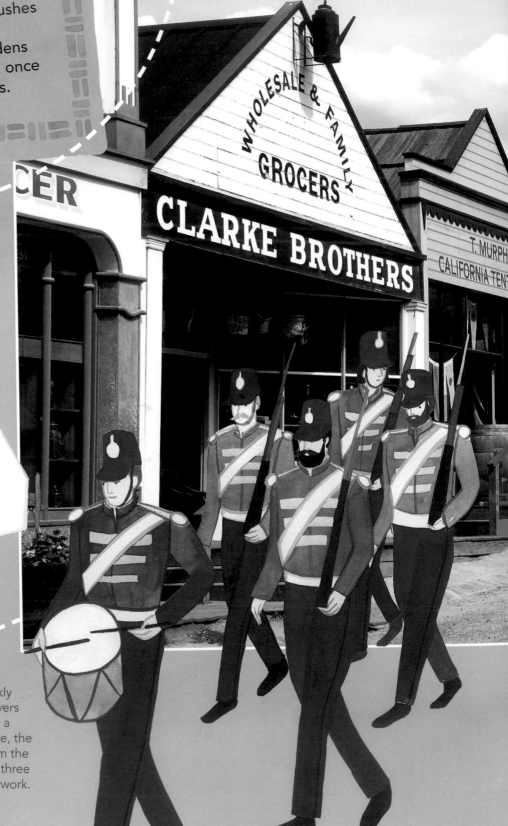

4 EUREKA!

When a digger was killed at the Eureka Hotel, and the presumed killer wasn't brought to justice, things turned violent. Men grabbed their guns and built a stockade, making a circle out of wooden stakes and horse-carts. The miners swore allegiance to the Eureka flag – a white cross and stars on a blue background. On 3 December 1854, the government forces overran the stockade in a quick and bloody battle. In ten minutes, as many as 34 miners were left dead or wounded. The rebellion was over.

SOVEREIGN HILL

Ballarat was so shaped by its glittering past, in 1970 it decided to build a full-scale replica Gold Rush town complete with shops, schools and underground mines. Sovereign Hill is an amazing outdoor museum, offering a glimpse of city life in those crazy, strike-it-rich-quick days. Visitors can pan for real gold, explore the dusty streets, or take a ride in a horse-drawn coach.

5 ALL THAT FOR NOTHING?

The Eureka stockade deaths weren't completely in vain, however. Three years later the Victorian Parliament gave the vote to all white men in the colony, a move that could have been a direct result of the uprising. Today the Museum of Australian Democracy (MADE) stands on the site of Eureka Rebellion. It looks back at the rebellion as an inspiring example of people bravely taking matters into their own hands when they felt that justice wasn't being done.

BALLARAT NOW

Modern Ballarat is a peaceful, provincial city. Although the gold is long gone, there are still many signs of those dramatic early days. The centre of town is lined with grand, Victorian buildings and there are monuments and memorials all across Ballarat that honour the bravery of the rebels. Even now, the Eureka flag is still flown.

MELBOURNE

AUSTRALIA Oceania

Melbourne is one of a kind – a proud Australian city with a cool, European vibe. Despite its short history, Melbourne has made a name for itself as a prosperous town that loves its art and its sport in equal measure. Children squeal with giggles at the Luna Park funfair, trams click up and down the streets and boats cruise along the Yarra River.

THE WORLD COMES TO STAY

Ever since it was first founded by British immigrants and convicts, Melbourne has been a migrant city. Today it's more like a world in miniature, with huge populations from Greece, Italy, China, Lebanon, Vietnam, Turkey, India, Sri Lanka, Ethiopia, Somalia, Malaysia, Indonesia and elsewhere. Over 200 countries are represented in the metropolis and more than a quarter of all Melburnians were born overseas.

WHERE BIRDS DON'T FLY...

Australia has plenty of emus and cassowaries, but there is another type of flightless bird that is unique to Melbourne – the Moomba Birdman. Every March, Birdmen kitted out in fantastic homemade planes and gliders launch themselves off a pontoon to see who can fly the furthest across the Yarra River. Virtually all of the Birdmen just flop hopelessly into the water, but that doesn't stop them trying again, year after year. Moomba, by the way, means 'up your bum'. Rumour has it that local Aboriginal people suggested the name as a joke and now it seems that Melbourne is stuck with it!

...BUT LUNCH DOES

Melbourne has one of the weirdest food delivery systems in the world – the jafflechute. A jafflechute is a curious thing! It's made up of a toasted sandwich (known as a 'jaffle' in and around Melbourne) and a parachute. Hungry customers order online and arrange a time to pick up their sandwich. When they're ready to eat, they go and stand on an 'X' painted on the pavement below jafflechute headquarters. After a little while their lunch simply floats down from the building above. Easy!

WILLIAM BUCKLEY

William Buckley was brought to Victoria from England as a convict in 1803, but took his chances and escaped into the bush. He lived for the next 32 years with a local Aboriginal tribe, the Wathaurung people. When Europeans returned to establish the 'Port Philip District' (as Melbourne was first called), they were astonished to come across Buckley dressed in kangaroo skins. The chances of an English man surviving in the bush for all of those years were so small that people in Melbourne still tell each other, 'you've got Buckley's chance'. It's as good as saying that you've got almost no chance at all!

SPORT CENTRAL

Melbourne is crazy about sport. Australia's biggest game, Australian Rules Football (AFL), was invented here and half of the top 18 teams in the country are based in the city. The AFL's most important matches are played at the Melbourne Cricket Ground, the country's biggest and most famous sports stadium. The MCG was also the venue for the first ever cricket Test match, held between Australia and England. But that's only for starters! The Australian Open tennis, the Australian Formula One Grand Prix, the Melbourne Cup (Australia's biggest horse race) and a dozen other big-ticket events show just how deep the passion goes.

MELBOURNE IN 38,000 BC

Melbourne's modern history only goes back to 1835, but there have been people living here for a little longer than that – around 40,000 years longer! The Kulin Nation, a confederation of five different Aboriginal tribes, have called this country home since the days before the rise and fall of Egypt, Mesopotamia or in fact any other ancient civilisation.

LANES, GRAFFITI, AND CAFÉS

Melbourne is known for its arty, laidback atmosphere. It feels as if there is a café on every corner, bustling with locals sitting down to coffee and fancy breakfasts. The centre of town is criss-crossed with vibrant little lanes that feel more like outdoor art galleries than streets. The city actively encourages graffiti artists to decorate the bare bricks with vibrant murals and scenes. People fly in from all around the world to admire their work.

SYDNEY
AUSTRALIA Oceania

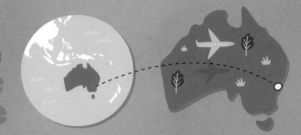

Sydney is the undisputed jewel in Australia's crown. The beautiful metropolis curves around the largest natural harbour in the world. Iconic landmarks sparkle in the sunshine, beaches bustle with surfers and restaurants serve up fabulous fusion food. All the while the vibrant, diverse Sydneysiders go about their daily lives.

MRS MACQUARIE'S CHAIR

SYDNEY OPERA HOUSE

SYDNEY HARBOUR BRIDGE

MRS MACQUARIE'S CHAIR

One of the best views across the city has to be from Mrs Macquarie's Point, on the eastern edge of the Royal Botanic Gardens. In 1810, Governor Lachlan Macquarie had a stone chair carved out of a sandstone rock ledge for his wife, Elizabeth. It is said that the lady liked to sit there and look out for British ships sailing into the harbour. She chose well – from the chair you can see the Sydney Harbour Bridge, Navy dockyards and even the mountains in the distance.

PORT JACKSON

SYDNEY

THE HARBOUR

Port Jackson, which includes Sydney Harbour, Middle Harbour and North Harbour, is the world's deepest natural harbour. At its deepest, between Dawes Point and Blues Point, it's 47m (154ft) down to the bottom. The harbour is so important to Sydney's fortunes, many simply refer to it as the 'Harbour City'.

SHOCK OPERA

The now much-loved Sydney Opera House was seriously shocking when it first opened in 1973. No one in the city had ever erected such a bizarre public building! The shell rooftops are covered with more than a million white tiles, shaped to look like a series of sails. Inside the structure there are seven concert venues and a thousand rooms. The design was the result of a competition, with the architect Jørn Utzon earning a £5,000 prize for his winning entry.

ROYAL
BOTANIC
GARDENS

DARLING
HARBOUR

CIRCULAR
QUAY

ALL CHANGE

The Harbour has seen a lot of change over the past 200 years and it's still on the move today. Take Darling Harbour, for example. Once it was a working port in the heart of Sydney, full of wharves, docks, sheds and railway tracks. Now it's a huge entertainment complex, complete with a casino, an aquarium, museums and shopping centres. It can even boast the world's largest cinema screen!

GLOBAL SUPERSTAR

When the Sydney Harbour Bridge opened in 1932, it was both the widest long span and the highest steel arch bridge in the world. The giant feat of engineering holds up the very heart of the city, connecting the towering business district with the teeming suburbs of the North Shore. On calm days, brave visitors can put on harnesses and climb right up to the 134m (440ft) summit. Every New Year's Eve, the bridge becomes the focal point of a jaw-dropping fireworks display, watched by millions of viewers all over the world.

SAILING TO SCHOOL

The Harbour isn't just beautiful – it's the centre of everyday life in Sydney. Thousands of people criss-cross the deep blue to get to and from work, school and home. While some have their own boats, for most this means making use of Sydney's ferries. The main hub is at Circular Quay, tucked in between the Bridge and the Opera House. A steady stream of ferries make their way out to Manly, Taronga Zoo, Parramatta and other famous parts of the city.

SYDNEY

Sydney is such a powerful emblem of Australia, many expect it to be the capital rather than Canberra. What the city lacks in status however, it more than makes up for in size. Today a staggering 20 per cent of the Australian population are lucky enough to call Sydney home.

LOCAL LINGO

Most of the land that Sydney now stands first belonged to the Eora people. Their descendants still live on in the area, dispersed amongst 29 different clans. Eora rock art is scattered across secret locations throughout the city, some of it painted tens of thousands of years ago. While the Eora resisted the first settlers, they also provided them with a language to describe the weird and wonderful things that they encountered in this strange, new land. 'Wallaby', 'dingo' and 'wombat' are just some of the words the Eora added to the English dictionary.

SWANKY SYDNEY

Sydney has a reputation for being the most glamorous city in Australia. Its stunning waterside location, extravagant buildings and great restaurants attract the nation's rich and famous. And, as the rich and famous tend to do, they've built themselves some pretty nice places to sleep. Australia's most expensive houses gleam above the rocks along the best sections of shore that the city has to offer. There are huge, luxurious mansions that come with private beaches, tennis courts and of course, swimming pools as standard.

PARTY TOWN

This city loves a party! All through the year there are events dedicated to food, culture and much more. Vivid Sydney is the world's biggest festival of lights, music and ideas. Every winter the city is transformed in a shimmer of beams, lanterns and neon. Light sculptures pop up in public spaces, crowds gather for interactive displays and amazing shapes are projected onto Sydney's most iconic landmarks.

SUNNY CHRISTMAS

Sydney is known around the world for its beaches, but Bondi is surely the most famous of them all. The holiday hotspot is in the east of the city, where the Pacific Ocean creates great, tumbling waves. Bondi isn't just about swimming, however. The beach also hosts regular art shows, kite flying festivals and city to surf running marathons. On Christmas Day, it is the tradition for local families to put on their santa hats and celebrate on the beach.

AUSTRALIA DAY

On 26 January every year, Australia Day, the city commemorates the arrival of the first fleet from Great Britain. Captain Arthur Philip was at the helm of *HMS Sirius*, a ship commissioned to transport convicts to the Southern Hemisphere. After eight hard months on the water, *Sirius* finally landed in Sydney Cove. That was way back in 1788 – today it's a national holiday marked by thousands of fluttering red, white and blue flags. Aboriginal elders also lead ceremonies to honour the ancient heritage of Australia.

OLYMPIC CITY

Sydney's finest moment in the sun was probably the 2000 Olympic Games. As soon as the city won the bid in 1993, its planners swung into action. A massive program of building and preparation began, that would eventually set the city back £3.2 billion. When the Games finally arrived however, Sydney was ready to put on a show. Over 10,000 athletes competed in 300 different events and 6.7 million tickets were sold. Sports fans and commentators queued up to declare Sydney 2000 the most successful games in Olympic history.

AUCKLAND
NEW ZEALAND Oceania

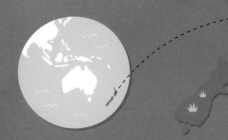

Auckland is New Zealand's biggest city. And while it's not the capital – that honour goes to Wellington – many say that it's the most welcoming. The City of Sails embraces people from Tonga, Samoa and Fiji, and has the biggest Polynesian population of any city in the world. Together with a growing Asian community and the native Maori people, Auckland has a vibrant, international feel.

MAORI PA

According to Maori legend, the fertile soils and volcanic peaks of the Auckland area were created when two *iwi* (tribes) clashed many centuries ago. The Maori built forts, called *pa*, on volcanic hills around the city, which were then terraced and reinforced by the *iwi*. While many of them are no more than grassy mounds today, they give a sense of how powerful and complex the Maori civilization was before the Europeans invaded.

GOVERNOR GEORGE GREY

Governor George Grey was no ordinary politician. By the age of 27, he had led two expeditions into Western Australia, had been shipwrecked and then survived only by drinking liquid mud. He moved to Auckland in 1845 and governed New Zealand until 1853, taking the reins of power back up again between 1861 and 1868. Grey brought order to the country and initially won the hearts of the Maori with his interest in their customs and beliefs – although he later fought multiple land wars against them. Aucklanders strolling through Albert Park can pay their respects to Grey by visiting his marble statue.

CITY OF SAILS

Auckland sits on a stretch of land surrounded by the Waitemata and Manukau harbours, with access to the Tasman Sea. The waterfront is a forest of masts – with countless yachts, schooners, dinghies and catamarans bobbing side by side. Auckland truly deserves its nickname! There are more boats per person here than in any other city in the world.

HILLARY'S HEAD FOR HEIGHTS

One of Auckland's most famous sons is Sir Edmund Hillary, the man who, along with Tenzing Norgay, was the first to scale Mount Everest. Hillary was born in Auckland in 1919 and also died in the city, in 2008. Since then, his achievements have been honoured in many ways. Exhibitions have been held at the Auckland museum, a track around the city's dramatic west coast called the Hillary Trail has been established and a retirement village has been named after the epic climber!

REACH FOR THE SKY

Auckland is home to the tallest manmade structure in the Southern Hemisphere, the awe-inspiring Sky Tower. Looking a bit like an alien spacecraft getting ready to return home from a mission to Earth, it's a 328m (1,076ft) high needle of a building, used for telecommunications and observation. The tower dominates Auckland's skyline, and many thrillseekers have used it for freefalling. They attach themselves to an elastic rope and then drop 192m (630ft) from the top. Extreme!

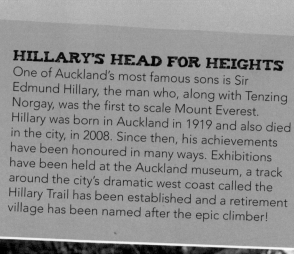

AMERICA'S CUP

It's no surprise that the Aucklanders love sailing and there's one prize that all of them want to win – the America's Cup. If excitement was high in Auckland during 1995, when Team NZ won for the first time, it was boiling over in 2000. The Cup was defended in Auckland itself with a sweeping, spectacular 5-nil victory over the Italian team.

BAREFOOT BALL SKILLS

Most young children in Auckland grow up running around without shoes. It's not because they can't afford them, it's because it feels comfortable! It is also believed to be healthier to allow young feet to grow naturally, without cramping them up in a shoe. Although many primary schools in Auckland now require footwear to be worn during the day, lots of kids still walk to and from class barefoot as well as removing their shoes during playtime. They even play barefoot sevens rugby!

ROTORUA
NEW ZEALAND Oceania

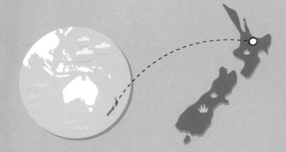

Rotorua is one of New Zealand's most popular tourist destinations, and no wonder! Spectacular natural marvels combine with living Maori culture to make it an amazing place to visit. Rotorua is an awesome place to live, too, with forests full of bike trails, a cool lake scene and an extreme sports park right on its doorstep.

THE HEAT BENEATH YOUR FEET

New Zealand stretches across a tectonic subduction zone. That's a fancy way of describing a place where one piece of the earth (the Pacific Plate) slides under another (the Australian Plate). Wherever this happens, there is an explosion of volcanoes, earthquakes and other geothermal activity. Heat rises up from under the ground all over Rotorua, creating churning mud pools, geysers, hot springs and other weird phenomena.

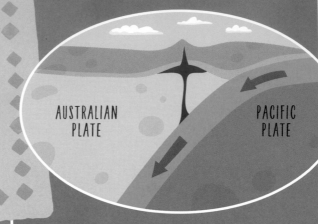

AUSTRALIAN PLATE

PACIFIC PLATE

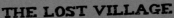

THE LOST VILLAGE

All New Zealanders know that the volatile forces beneath their feet can sometimes turn treacherous. This was never clearer than on 10 June 1886, when Mount Tarawera, a volcano just 20km (12mi) from Rotorua, erupted. Waves of boiling mud poured down the mountain, burying the tiny village of Te Waiora and killing over 150 people. It wasn't until the 1930s that the lost buildings began to be resurrected again. Today visitors can go to Te Waiora and see how life was lived before the village was claimed by the uneasy earth.

THE GREAT OUTDOORS

Children growing up in Rotorua spend a lot of time outdoors. The region around that city is dotted with lakes that are perfect for swimming and waterskiing. In the Redwoods forest there are also hundreds of kilometres of trails to hike along. The city even has its own special extreme sports park. At Agroventures, visitors can soar through the air on a sky swing, freefall in a wind tunnel and take a breathless ride around a pedal-powered monorail track.

WHAKAREWAREWA

This smoke-strewn, eerie landscape, pronounced 'fa-ka-re-wa-re-wa', is one of the most active geothermal sites in New Zealand. It bubbles with over 500 hot springs and 65 geysers – vents in the earth that regularly spew out hot water and steam, set against terraces of rock in lurid yellows, reds and browns. The Maori village in Whakarewarewa has a proud heritage. The Tuhourangi/Ngati Wahiao people have lived here for over 700 years.

GLORIOUS MUD

The Maori people have been making use of the city's geothermal wonders for hundreds of years, especially for cooking and bathing. Now many local and overseas visitors also come to the city for some health and relaxation, Rotorua-style. They bathe in hot springs, slap mud onto their bodies and even drink the smelly, mineral-rich water. It's said to be very good for you!

HELL'S GATE

Hell's Gate is not as nasty as it sounds, but it is a great place to get dirty! The geothermal park has its very own 18m (59ft) high mud volcano that erupts every six weeks or so. Every time the cone blows its top, mud bombs are thrown into the air and hot gunge oozes everywhere. The volcano grows a little bigger every time. Visitors to Hell's Gate love to give themselves icky, mud body treatments. There are three types to choose from – black, white or grey.

HUNGRY FOR A HANGI?

Hangi is the traditional Maori form of barbecuing. A pit is dug in the ground, the bottom is lined with heated stones, then the food is placed on top and covered with earth. Several hours later the meal is dug up, warm and ready to eat. The cooking stage doesn't take quite as long in Rotorua because the ground is already hot.

QUEENSTOWN
NEW ZEALAND Oceania

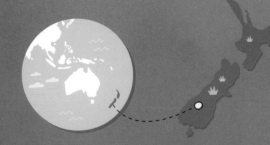

Queenstown's dramatic scenery is both otherworldly and world famous. The New Zealand director Sir Peter Jackson chose to set much of his *Hobbit* and *The Lord Of The Rings* trilogies in and around the area, bringing the city's beauty to the big screen. Queenstown is also a mecca for skiers and the home of the New Zealand Winter Games.

WILDLIFE PARADISE
Luckily the huge numbers of thrillseekers who visit Queenstown have not managed to chase away the wildlife. Chamois and red deer clamber and graze on the slopes, whilst massive locust-type creatures called weta share the rocks and crevices with giant weevils and rock skink lizards. New Zealand falcon, pipits and black-billed gulls swoop and dive through the skies above.

DOOMED GIANT
Queenstown sits on the edge of a clear, blue inland lake called Wakatipu. This stunning stretch of water was formed by glaciers cutting through the Southern Alps 15,000 years ago. According to Maori folklore however, the true story is quite different. Legend has it that Manata, the daughter of a local chief, was forbidden to marry her love, Matakauri. One night a giant named Matau kidnapped Manata and took her to his lair. Matakauri rescued the girl from the giant's clutches and the two were allowed to marry. Sadly there was no happy ending for the giant – to keep his new bride safe, Matakauri went back to Matau's lair and burned him where he lay. The fire seared a deep gouge into the earth, causing the ice and snow to melt and Lake Wakatipu to be formed. The name literally means 'Hollow of the Giant'.

THAT REMARKABLE NAME

Queenstown's most famous mountains are the Remarkables. No one's certain how they got their name – many claim that it was a term coined in 1857 by Alexander Garvie. Garvie was a European surveyor who was astonished to come across a mountain range that ran directly from north to south. Others say that early Queenstown settlers came up with the title after viewing the dramatic razorback mountain range at sunset. Whatever the truth, these spectacular peaks more than merit their 'remarkable' tag.

MIDDLE EARTH

When the makers of the epic *The Lord Of The Rings* films were looking for a backdrop that could evoke the fantasy land of Middle Earth, they came to Queenstown. The scenes of the camp in Dimrill Dale were filmed right there, in the awe-inspiring mountains. In fact, Queenstown is really one enormous movie set. Other nearby places featured in *The Lord Of The Rings* include Deer Park Heights, Lake Wakatipu, Glenorchy and Skippers Canyon. The Tolkien trilogies were a worldwide success, winning many Academy Awards.

SKI CENTRAL

With nearly 4m (13ft) of snow each year, the Remarkables aren't just for looking at – they're also for sliding down! Queenstown is New Zealand's busiest ski resort, packed with winter sports fans all season long. The really bold skiers and snowboarders hire helicopters to take them to the highest and wildest peaks. Once they have been dropped off, they crisscross down the Remarkables' most challenging runs, showing the others how it is done.

QUEENSTOWN

Queenstown isn't just about the gorgeous scenery. All sorts of people come to take advantage of everything that this small, but perfectly formed city has to offer. Gap year students raft down rapids and brave bungee jumps, wine-lovers tour the vineyards and families sunbathe and play along the sandy strip.

PARTY PEOPLE

One of the most amazing things about Queenstown is that it's as lively and buzzy in the winter as it is in the summer. Every year around 45,000 people descend on the city ready to celebrate the Winter Festival. There are fireworks, street parties, ice-skating, races down the mountain and concerts. In summer, the place throbs to the beat of countless music festivals held along the beaches, in the woodland and in Queenstown's parks.

YUM YUM

Forget McDonalds and Ben & Jerry's – local kids are more likely to head out for a Fergburger and some hokey pokey ice cream! Fergburger is a crazily named eaterie that started out as a hole-in-the-wall. Since then its burgers, including the Little Lamby and Mr Big Stuff, have made it a Queenstown legend. As for hokey pokey – it's the city's second most popular ice cream flavour after vanilla. Every scoop is full of crumbly honeycomb and toffee. Scrumptious!

MY, MY, MAORI

Maori culture is woven into modern life in Queenstown. Maori art and designs such as tiki pendants appear in galleries, studios and weekly craft markets. The traditions of the Maori are also celebrated daily in song and dance at the Kiwi Haka, a theatre overlooking the city.

BUNGEE, GLIDE OR ZIPLINE?

Bungee may not have been invented in Queenstown, but this is where it first became famous. The Kawarau Bridge is now one of the best-known bungee spots in the world, and at 134m (439ft), the Nevis Highwire is the highest. Of course, if hurtling towards the ground is not your thing, there's always soaring like a bird over Queenstown on a tandem paraglider, whitewater rafting on the Shotover River, or rushing through the air on a zipline. Eager riders whoosh along wires suspended high above the trees, spinning and turning as they go.

TREASURES BELOW

Queenstown didn't have to wait for 20th century adventure tourism to arrive in order to swell its numbers. For centuries, the Maori people have come to the city in search of jade. They know the mysterious green stone as *pounamu*. It is highly prized, especially when carved into intricate pieces that are passed down through the generations. In the 1860s the Otago Gold Rush also brought tens of thousands of prospectors to Queensland, hoping to plunder the glistening treasures hidden below Skippers Canyon.

A REAL TOURIST TOWN

It's not surprising that Queenstown, with its incredible natural beauty and all those opportunities for adventure, should attract a few visitors. What is staggering is the sheer number that flock to the city, compared to those who live there. Every year the 28,000 inhabitants are joined by as many as 1.8 million tourists. That's 64 out-of-towners for every person that permanently lives in Queenstown!

APIA

SAMOA Oceania

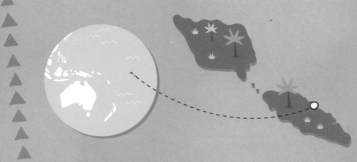

Once a tiny fishing village on the island of Upolu, Apia is now the capital of the Pacific nation of Samoa. It's not the biggest city – fewer than 40,000 people live there – but what Apia lacks in size, it more than makes up for in setting. The capital sits in a natural harbour lined with white sand beaches on one side and volcanic mountains on the other.

SHIPWRECK CITY

Apia harbour is a giant ships' graveyard. In 1889, when Germany, the United States and England stuck their oars into a dispute over the Samoans' choice of king, disaster struck. The standoff led all three major powers to anchor their warships in the harbour, refusing to move them even when a huge cyclone bore down on the city. In the end, only the English ship *HMS Calliope* managed to head to the safety of deeper water. The three German and three American ships were all wrecked where they were moored. Their rusted remains still litter the water today.

CANOES AND STARS

Apia really is a long way from anywhere. Even today, travellers have to sit on a plane for hours, or ride in a boat for days, just to get there. Imagine the journey of the first settlers, 3,000 years ago! The Polynesians came from Asia, thousands of kilometres away. They rode in canoes carved out of hollow trees, using the stars to navigate. The Samoans retain their incredible seafaring skills to this day, thinking nothing of steering tiny boats out of Apia harbour into the colossal swell of the Pacific Ocean.

FA'A SAMOA

Apia might be a modern capital city, but the traditional way of life, the Fa'a Samoa (Samoan Way), still carries on. In Apia, it is important to remove your shoes before entering a *fale* (traditional house) and to wait until elders are seated before sitting down yourself, always making sure that your feet aren't pointing directly at anybody. Until 1860, Samoan villages like Apia were ruled by chiefs called *matai*, who were responsible for their *aiga* (extended family). Samoa may have a modern government now, but the *matai* are still very powerful, even in today's Apia.

THE REAL TREASURE ISLAND?

Robert Louis Stevenson, the British author of *Treasure Island*, loved Samoa. In 1890 he moved to a house just outside the city called Villa Vailima. The Apians took Stevenson into their hearts, giving him the Samoan name *Tusitala*, meaning 'Storyteller'. The author spent the last four years of his life in Apia and was eventually buried on Mount Vaea, the 472m (1,549ft) jungle-clad peak that towers over the city.

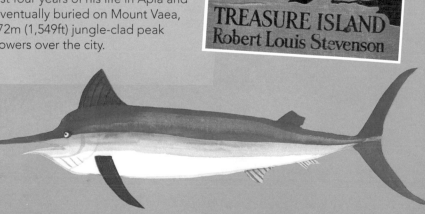

TREASURE ISLAND
Robert Louis Stevenson

WIND PROBLEMS

Each year between November and April Apians live in fear of one of nature's most violent phenomena – the tropical cyclone. Feeding on low pressure in the atmosphere and spinning either clockwise in the Southern Hemisphere or counter-clockwise in the Northern, these are storms on a mighty scale. Tropical cyclones can produce winds of up to 250 kph (153 mph), massive rainfall and flooding. Particularly bad cyclones hit Apia in 1889, 1990, 1991 and 2012. No one knows when the next big one will come.

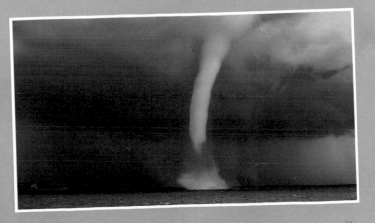

FISH SUPPERS

It's not surprising that the Samoans, living smack-bang in the middle of the world's biggest ocean, eat a lot of fish. The fish market is one of the busiest places in town, where all kinds of good things pulled straight from the sea are laid out, super-fresh and gleaming for shoppers to admire. Tuna and octopus are common sights, but there are also eels, black marlin and sea cucumber gizzards!

SOUTH TARAWA
KIRIBATI Oceania

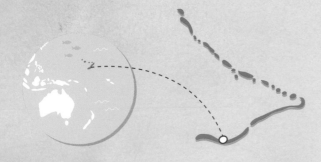

Have you ever heard of Kiribati, a country made up of tiny atolls (coral islands) in the Pacific Ocean? Its capital is South Tarawa – one of the most unusual cities in the world. South Tarawa only covers a tiny stretch of land, but it is packed with people. Many live in traditional open-sided huts just a stone's throw away from the big blue.

AEROPLANE FOOD
Salt water, sand and isolation don't make for the best farming conditions. While South Tarawa enjoys all the fish and coconut it can handle, everything else has to be flown or shipped in.

FANCY SWIMMING TO SCHOOL?
South Tarawa isn't like most cities. It's made up of 16 islets strung out across the 35km (22mi) long Tarawa Lagoon. There are really little ones (like Tangintebu, with only 89 people living on it) and not-so-little ones (like Betio, which has over 15,000). Together they make up one, watery city. Luckily residents don't have to dodge the sharks to get around – a causeway connects up all 16.

THE HIGHEST POINT OF SOUTH TARAWA

3 METRES

HOLDING BACK THE SEA
South Tarawa is really flat – the islands only rise 3m (9.84ft) above sea level. As global warming pushes the sea levels up soon that may not be high enough for everyone to stay dry. If the city does go under, the population of Kiribati will be forced to move to Australia, New Zealand, Fiji or one of its other Pacific neighbours.

BATTLE OF TARAWA
This sleepy city hasn't always been so quiet. For 76 hours in November 1943, a terrible battle was fought between the Japanese and Americans for control of its little patches of sand in the sea. At this stage of World War Two, the Japanese were slowly losing their bid for the Pacific while the Americans wanted South Tarawa as an airfield. They got what they wanted, but only after more than 6,000 people died.

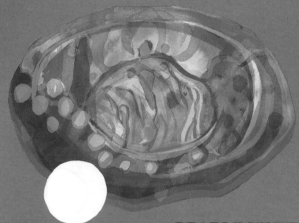

PEARLY WHITES
Aside from *copra* (dried coconut), South Tarawa's big money-spinner is *nacre*, or mother-of-pearl. The beautiful, rainbow-coloured shells in which the pearls grow were once considered more valuable than the pearls themselves. It is said that the children of South Tarawa once used to play marbles with the pearls that their parents threw away!

REMEMBER THE 12TH OF JULY
South Tarawa has a party each year when it celebrates its Independence Day. The *botaki* (celebration) includes feasts, singing, dancing, canoe racing and a unique sport called *oreano*. Teams throw super-heavy balls at each other, hoping that their opponents can't catch them!

INDEX

PICTURE CREDITS

The publisher would like to thank the following for their kind permission to reproduce their photographs:

Key: (a) above; (b) below/bottom; (c) centre; (f) far; (l) left; (r) right; (t) top.

Front Cover (tl): Shutterstock / my summit; (cr) Shutterstock / Peera_stockfoto; (cl) Shutterstock / Michele Alfieri.

Back Cover (tr): Shutterstock / Luciano Mortula; (cl): Getty Images / Grant Duncan Smith; (cr): Getty Images / LOOK-foto / Holger Leue; (bl): Alamy / Iamgestate Media Partners Limited – Impact Photos; (bc): Getty Images / Sebastian D'Souza.

P6 (t): Getty Images / Maria Swärd; P6 (bl): Getty Images / Brazil Photos; P7 (br): Getty Images / Education Images; P8 (tr): Getty Images / Carlos Osorio; P8 (cr) Shutterstock / Hurst Photo; P9 (tl): Alamy / Alan Novelli; P9 (cl): courtesy of CN Tower Media Centre; P9 (cr): Getty Images / Roberto Machado Noa; P9 (b): Shutterstock / rmnoa357; P10 (br): Getty Images / AFP / Olivier Jean; P11 (c): Shutterstock / bonchan; P11 (bc): Alamy / Marc Bruxelle; P12 (cl): Getty Images / Wolfgang Kaehler; P13 (tl): Alamy / icpix_can; P13 (tr): Shutterstock / FotoRequest; P13 (br): Alamy / Laurent Lucuix; P13 (bl): Shutterstock / Thomas Brain; Pages 14–15 (t): Getty Images / Wolfgang Kaehler; P14 (l): Shutterstock / 2009fotofriends; P14 (br): Shutterstock / Josef Hanus; P15 (cr): Alamy / Chris Cheadle; P16 (tr): Getty Images / The Print Collector; P17 (tl): Getty Images / NYPL / Science Source; P17 (tr): Getty Images / Holger Leue / LOOK-foto; P17 (b): Getty Images / Angelique Shepherd; P18 (cr): Alamy / GoUSA; P18 (cl): Getty Images / Luis Sinco; P18 (br): Shutterstock / Maxx-Studio; P19 (tl): Shutterstock / littleny; P19 (tr): Getty Images / James Aylott; P19 (cl): Shutterstock / View Apart; P19 (br) HOLLYWOOD™ and design © 2016 Hollywood Chamber of Commerce. The Hollywood Sign is a trademark and the intellectual property of Hollywood Chamber of Commerce. All Rights Reserved. P20 (tr): Getty Images / Ethan Miller; P20 (bla): Shutterstock / welcomia; P20 (blb): Shutterstock / Gary Paul Lewis; P20 (br): Getty Images / Steven Lawton; P21 (tl): Getty Images / Samuel Antonio; P21 (cr): Alamy / Danita Delimont; P22 (tr): Shutterstock / Art_man; P22 (cl): Getty Images / Buyenlarge / Carol M. Highsmith; P22 (cr): Alamy / PHOTOTAKE Inc.; P23 (tr): Getty Images / NOAA; P23 (tl): Getty Images / Mark Wilson; P23 (bl): Getty Images / Dave Einsel; P23 (br): Getty Images / AFP / Pool; P24 (cr): Alamy / Brian Jannsen; P24 (br): Shutterstock / Jeffrey M. Frank; P25 (t): Alamy / Paul Briden; P25 (bl): Alamy / Niday Picture Library; P26 (tr): Getty Images / George Rose; P26 (cr): Shutterstock / Tupungato. Artist: Anish Kapoor; P26 (bl): Getty Images / Joe Robbins; P26 (br): Alamy / Ian Dagnal; P27 (tl): Alamy / Niday Picture Library; P27 (c): Shutterstock / saraporn; P27 (cr): Alamy / Gino's Premium Images; P28 (tr): Getty Images / AFP / Stan Honda; P28 (cl): Getty Images / Ben Hider; P28 (br): Getty Images / The Boston Globe / David L. Ryan; P29 (tl): Getty Images / Education Images; P29 (bl): Getty Images / Jeroen Peis; P29 (br): Shutterstock / TerraceStudio; P30 (br): Alamy / Chase Guttman; P30 (bl): Getty Images / AFP / Emmanuel Dunand; P31 (tr): Getty Images / AFP / Ben Stanstall; P31 (tl): Shutterstock / Stuart Monk; P31 (cr): Getty Images / AFP / Jung Yeon-Je; P32 (cr): Alamy / B. O'Kane; P32 (bl): Getty Images / Buyenlarge / Carol M. Highsmith; P32 (br): Getty Images / Allentown Morning Call / Harry Fisher; P33 (t): Getty Images / Classic Stock / H. Armstrong Roberts; P33 (cl): Getty Images / Todd Gipstein; P33 (bl): Getty Images / Bruce Yuanye Bi; P34 (r): Getty Images / Dennis K. Johnson; P34 (c): Getty Images / AFP / Brendan Smialowski; P35 (cl): Getty Images / Kris Connor; P35 (cr): Getty Images / The Washington Post / Marvin Joseph; P35 (br) Getty Images / bbourdages; P36 (tr): Corbis / Richard Cummins; P36 (cl): Getty Images / Carol Grant; P36 (b): Getty Images / Cultura RM / Art Wolfe Stock; P37 (tl): Shutterstock / Boris Vetshev; P37 (cl): Getty Images / Ra\'id Khalil; P37 (b): Alamy / Buddy Mays; P37 (br): Getty Images / John Elk II; Pages 38–39 (t): Getty Images / Patrik Bergström; P38 (bl): Shutterstock / Filipe Frazao; P38 (br): Getty Images / Christopher Groenhout; P39 (br): Alamy / B. O'Kane; P40 (tr): Getty Images / PYMCA; P40 (bl): Corbis / JAI / Doug Pearson/ Artist: Laura Facey; P40 (br): Shutterstock / Vaide Seskauskiene; P41 (tl): Getty Images / John Greim; P41 (tr): Getty Images / AFP/ Mark Cardwell; P41 (bl): Getty Images / Peter Still; P42 (tr): Alamy / Edward Parker; P42 (bl): Shutterstock / Chepe Nicoli; P43 (t): Getty Images / trekholidays; P43 (b): Getty Images / Peter Macdiarmid; Pages 44–45 (t): Alamy Images / Richard Ellis; P44 (cl): Getty Images / Richard Ellis; P45 (br): Getty Images / Richard Ellis; Pages 46–47 (t): Shutterstock / Gary Yim; P46 (cr): Getty Images / John Coletti; P46 (bl): Alamy / EPA / Martin Alipaz; P47 (cr): Getty Images / John Coletti; P48 (tr): Shutterstock / Radu Bercan; P49 (tl): Alamy / dbimages; P49 (cr): Getty Images / Kaveh Kazemi; P49 (bl): Getty Images / Wolfgang Kaehler; P50 (cr): Getty Images / Marcelo Andre; P50 (b): Alamy / age fotostock; P51 (tr): Shutterstock / Marcos Amend; P51 (c): Shutterstock / Filipe Frazao; P51 (br): Alamy / GM Photo Images; Pages 52–53 (t): Getty Images / Brazil Photos / Ratao Diniz; P52 (bl): © ADAGP Paris and DACS London 2016 / Shutterstock / T. Photography; P53 (tr): Shutterstock / CP DC Press; Pages 52–53 (b): Shutterstock / trinidade51; P53 (bc): Alamy / Trinity Mirror / Mirrorpix; P54 (tr): Shutterstock / Gary Yim; P54 (cl): Getty Images / Jan Sochor; P55: Shutterstock / T. Photography; P56 (cl): Shutterstock / Matyas Rehak; P56 (b): Alamy / Frans Lemmens; P57 (t): Shutterstock / 3523studio; P57 (cr): Alamy / Ian Wood; P58 (t): Shutterstock / Rafael Martin-Gaitero; P58 (b): Alamy / UpperCut Images; P59 (t): Alamy / Efrain Padro; P59 (c): Shutterstock / sunsinger; P59 (b): Getty Images / Chad Ehlers; P60 (c): Shutterstock / LMspencer; P61 (tl): Alamy / Design Pics Inc; P61 (br): Alamy / National Geographic Creative; Pages 62–63 (t): Shutterstock / SurangaSL; P62 (cl): Shutterstock / J. Helgason; P62 (br): Shutterstock / Alexei Stiop; P63 (cl): Alamy / Ashley Cooper; P63 (br): Shutterstock / Bernhard Richter; P64 (c): Getty Images / Lars Thulin; P64 (b): Getty Images / Rosita So Image; P65: Getty Images / Mike Hill; P66 (cr): Alamy / INTERFOTO; P67 (tl): Alamy / VPC Photo; P67 (tr): Shutterstock / andregric; P67 (bl): Shutterstock / Stefan Holm; P67 (br): Getty Images / JOKER / Paul Eckenroth. Artist: Peter Varhelyi; P68 (tr): Getty Images / MyLoupe; P68 (cl): Shutterstock / Verkhovynets Taras; P69 (tr): Getty Images / Stephen Dalton; P69 (cr): Shutterstock / Craig Russell; P69 (br): Getty Images / De Agostini / A. Dagli Orti/ Artist: Alice Eriksen; P70 (tr): Shutterstock / Juriaan Wossink; P70 (cr): Shutterstock / bonchan; P70 (bl): Shutterstock / Jan Kranendonk; P71 (tr): Getty Images / Jeff J. Mitchell; P71 (tl): Alamy / Design Pics Inc; P71 (cl): Getty Images / David C. Tomlinson; P71 (b): Getty Images / Izzet Keribar; P72 (tr): Shutterstock / s_oleg; P72 (c): Shutterstock / Kiev.Victor; P72 (bl): Shutterstock / r.nagy; P72 (br): Shutterstock / chrisdorney; P73 (tl): Shutterstock / Leonid Andronov; P73 (cr): Getty Images / Oli Scarff; P73 (c): Getty Images / Vladimir Zakharov; P73 (bl): Shutterstock / Chris Jenner; P73 (br): Shutterstock / Juan Carlos Tinjaca; P74 (t): Getty Images / GraphicaArtis and Shutterstock / Alina Cardiae Photography; P74 (bl): Alamy / Imagestate Media Partners Ltd – Impact Photos; P74 (br): Alamy / Philip Pound; P75 (tl): Getty Images / John Turp; P75 (tr): Shutterstock / Ron Ellis; P75 (cl): Getty Images / Hulton Archive and Shutterstock / Alina Cardiae Photography; P75 (cr): Shutterstock / Claudio Divizia; P75 (br): Shutterstock / Anna Kucherova; P76 (cl): Shutterstock / islavicek; P76 (bl): Alamy / Design Pics Inc; P77 (tr): Getty Images / Photos.com; P77 (b): Alamy / Rik Hamilton; P78 (tr): Getty Images / Ullstein Bild; P78 (bl): Dreamstime / © Visual Skin; P78 (br): Getty Images / Photo 12; P79 (t): Alamy / Jason Langley; P80 (cr): Alamy / EPA / Stephanie Leco; P80 (bl): Shutterstock / josefkubes / Artist: Jijé; P81 (tl): Getty Images / Heidi Coppock-Beard; P81 (r): Getty Images / Krysztof Maczkowiak; P81 (cl): Getty Images / G.R. Richardson / Robert Harding; P82 (cl): Shutterstock / seen0001; P82 (cr): Shutterstock / Elena Schweitzer; P83 (tl): Shutterstock/ Ana del Castillo; P83 (tr): Shutterstock / mkmakingphotos; P83 (cl): Shutterstock / Denis Kuvaev; P84 (t): Shutterstock / Skreidzeleu; P85 (tl): Getty Images / Jean-Francois Deroubaix; P85 (cr): Getty Images / Francois Le Diascorn; P85 (bl): Alamy / Glenn Harper; P86 (c): Getty Images / Ullstein Bild; P86 (bl): Getty Images / Sean Gallup; With kind permission of AMPELMANN GmbH, www.ampelmann.de P87 (tl): Getty / Ullstein Bild; P87 (tr): Getty Images / Ullstein Bild; P87 (cl): Shutterstock / bonchan; P87 (cr): Getty Images / Ullstein Bild; P88 (cl): Shutterstock / aandoart; P88 (b): Shutterstock / Ninelle; P89 (t): Alamy / Mauritius Images GmbH; P89 (c): Getty Images / Laurie Noble; P90 (tr): Wawel Dragon sculpture, by Bronisław Chromy / Getty / Henryk T. Kaiser; P90 (br): Alamy / Pegaz; P91 (cr): Alamy / Paul Gapper; P91 (cl): Shutterstock / Radiokafka; P91 (b): Shutterstock / Dar1930; P92 (tr): Shutterstock / Vladimir Sazonov; P92 (cl): Shutterstock / kaprik; P92 (bc): Shutterstock / IgorGolovniov; P93 (t): Shutterstock / Sergey_Bogomyako; P93 (bl): Shutterstock / anyaivanova; P93 (br): Alamy / CTK Photo / Josef Horazny; sculptor: David Černy Pages 94–95 (t): Getty Images / Alexander Hassenstein; P94 (cl): Alamy / Vidura Luis Barrios; P94 (cr): Getty Images / Three Lions; P94 (bl): Getty Images / Imagno; P95 (tr): Shutterstock / studiogi; P96 (c): Shutterstock / Ilyas Kalimullin; P96 (cr): Shutterstock /anshar: P96 (b): Shutterstock / JevgenjisB; P97 (cl): Shutterstock / Vitaly Korovin; P97 (cr): Getty Images / AFP /Kirill Kudryavtsev; P97 (b): Shutterstock / VLADJ55; P98 (tr): Shutterstock / KKulikov; P98 (cr): Shutterstock / Ekaterina Bykova; P98 (bl): Shutterstock / Irina Afonskaya; P98 (br): Alamy / SPUTNIK; P99 (tl): Shutterstock / danilov; P99 (b): Shutterstock / Triff; P100 (tr): Alamy / kpzfoto; P100 (cl): Shutterstock / Hellen Sergeyeva; P100 (br): Shutterstock / Sergey Kamshylin; P101 (tc): Getty Images / AFP / Genya Savilov; P101 (cl): Alamy / RGB Ventures / Superstock; P101 (clb): Corbis / EPA / Tatyana Zenkovich; P101: (bc): Shutterstock / Luuk de Kok; P101 (br): Getty Images / Sean Gallup; P102–103 (tc): Shutterstock / seqoya; P102 (bl): Shutterstock / Artur Bogacki; P103 (tr): Shutterstock / saiko3p; P103 (cr): Alamy / Hackenberg-Photo-Cologne; P103 (b): Shutterstock / JM Travel Photography; P104 (cr): Getty Images / Anadolu Agency; P104 (bl): Getty Images / Anadolu Agency; P105 (tr): Alamy / Claudia Wiens; P105 (br): Shutterstock / Sadik Gulek; P106 (c): Getty Images / DeAgostini / S. Vannini; P106 (bc): Alamy / AegeanPhoto; P107 (t): Shutterstock / Nick Pavlakis; P107 (cl): Shutterstock / Milan Gonda; P107 (br): Shutterstock / Anastasios71; P108 (tr): Shutterstock / Matteo Gabrieli; P108 (c): Shutterstock / Viacheslav Lopatin; P109 (tr): Shutterstock / TTstudio; P109 (tl): Shutterstock / Sorin Colac; P109 (br): Shutterstock / Andrei Nekrassov; P109 (bl): Alamy / colaimages; P110 (cl): Alamy / DPA Picture Alliance; P110 (bl): Shutterstock / Irina Mos; P110 (br): Shutterstock / Route 66; P111 (tr): Getty Images / AFP / Filippo Monteforte; P111 (cr): Getty Images / AFP / Andreas Solaro; P111 (br): Alamy / Guido Vermeulen-Perdaen; P112 (cl): Shutterstock / StefanZZ; P112 (bc); Getty Images / Marco Secchi; P113 (tr): Shutterstock / Phillip Minnis; P113 (cr): Shutterstock / alexeleny; P114 (tl): Shutterstock / Boris-B; P114 (b): Shutterstock / Pecold; P115 (tr): Shutterstock / Deamles for Sale; P115 (bl): Shutterstock / Radu Rasvan / P116 (tr): Getty Images / John Greim; P116 (cl): Getty Images / JMN; P116 (b): Shutterstock / NaughtyNut; P117 (cr): Alamy / Maria Galan; P117 (bl): Shutterstock / Iakov Filimonov; P118 (b): Shutterstock / r.nagy; P119 (tr): Shutterstock / tkemot; P119 (cl): Shutterstock / nito; P119 (bc): Getty Images / David Ramos; P119 (br): Shutterstock / Ralf Siemieniec; P120 (cr): Getty Images / UIG / Education Images; P120 (bl): Shutterstock / jiawangkun; P121 (tl): Shutterstock / Goran Bogicevic; P121 (cr): Alamy / RobertHarding; P121 (bl): Shutterstock / Martin Lehmann; P122 (tr): Shutterstock / Maurizio De Mattei; P122 (cr): Shutterstock / Maurizio De Mattei; P122 (cl): Shutterstock / Christian Mueller; P123 (br): Shutterstock / Alessandro Coiro Mas; P124 (tr): Alamy / robertharding; P124 (bl): Getty Images / AFP / Marwan Naamani; P125 (tr): Shutterstock / eFesenko; P125 (tl): Alamy / Xinhua; P125 (br): Getty Images / Anadolu Agency; P126 (cl): Shutterstock / Anton_Ivanov; P126 (br): Alamy / The Print Collector; P127 (t): Alamy / Carolyn Clarke; P128 (tr): Getty Images / DeAgostini; G. Dagli Orti; P128 (bl): Getty Images / Insights; P129 (t): Alamy / dbimages; P129 (bl): Corbis / Charles & Josette Lenars; P129 (bc): Shutterstock / Eric Isselee; P130 (tr): Getty Images / AFP / Georges Gobet; P130 (cl): Shutterstock / Dereje; P130 (bc): Getty Images / Education Images; P131 (tr): Getty Images / AFP / Philippe Desmazes; P131 (cr): Designer/architect Pierre Goudiaby Atepa / Alamy / Friedrich Stark; P131 (bl): Shutterstock / antpun; P132 (cl): Getty Images / De Agostini Picture Library; P132 (c): Shutterstock / Dave Montreuil; P132 (b): Shutterstock / Dereje; P133 (t): Shutterstock / Aleksandr Hunta; P133 (c): Alamy / Patrizia Wyss; P133 (br): Shutterstock / Valentin Valkov; P134 (tl): Getty Images / AFP / Simon Maina; Pages 134–135 (t): Getty Images / Peter Macdiarmid; P135 (br): Shutterstock / Martin Mecnarowski; P136 (tr): Alamy / John Warburton-Lee Photography; P136 (cl): Alamy / Ariadne Van Zandbergen; P136 (br): Getty Images / Eric Lafforgue; P137 (tr): Shutterstock / danm12; P137 (tl): Shutterstock / Magdalena Paluchowska; P138 (tr): Getty Images / Grant Duncan Smith; P138 (cl): Alamy / EPA; P138 (bl): Shutterstock / EcoPrint; P139 (tr): Shutterstock / Renee Vititoe; P139 (tl): Alamy / LH Images; P139 (c): Getty Images / espiegle; P139 (bc): Alamy / Premium Stock Photography GmbH; P139 (br): Getty Images / Thomas Imo; P140 (tr): Getty Images / Hoberman Collection; P140 (cl): Shutterstock / DWaschnig; P140 (cr): Alamy / Eric Nathan; P140 (bl): Getty Images / jaz_bennett; P141 (br): Getty Images / wildestanimal; P142 (tr): Shutterstock / ChameleonsEye; P142 (b): Alamy / Ageev Rostislav; P143 (tr): Alamy / Tony Roddam; P143 (b): Shutterstock / Alexey Stiop; P144 (tr): Getty Images / Anadolu Agency; P144 (cl): Shutterstock / Kobby Dagan; P145 (tr): Shutterstock / Borya Galperin; P145 (bl): Shutterstock / suronin; P146 (tr): Getty Images / Kami Kami; Pages 146–147 (b): Getty Images / Issam Madkouk; P147 (cr): Getty Images / prmustafa; P147 (bl): Getty Images / Kami Kami; P148: (tl): Shutterstock / S-F; P148 (tr): Shutterstock / Sorbis; P149 (br): Shutterstock / Kotsovolos Panagiotis; P150 (c): Alamy / Tuul and Bruno Morandi; P151 (tr): Alamy / SFM GM WORLD; P151 (c): Alamy / Hemis; P151 (br): Shutterstock / Milosz Maslanka; P152 (cl): Alamy / Galit Seligmann; P152 (b): Getty Images / UIG; P153 (t): Getty Images / AFP / Sebastian D'Souza; P153 (bl): Shutterstock / Robin Kay; P154 (tr): Shutterstock / Alexandra Lande; P154 (bl): Getty Images / Pacific Press; P155 (tr): Alamy / David Pearson; P155 (bl): Alamy / Jorge Royan; P155 (br): Shutterstock / neelsky; P156 (cl): Getty Images / Kateryna Negoda; P156 (br): Shutterstock / Jesse33; P157 (tl): Alamy / Spring Images; P157 (br): Alamy / ImageBROKER; P158 (r): Alamy / Friedrich Stark; P159 (tl): Alamy / Roberto Esposti; P159 (cl): Getty Images / ChinaFotoPress; P159 (br): Getty Images / samafoto; P160 (tr): Shutterstock / feiyuezhangjie; P160 (cl): Shutterstock / ChameleonsEye; P161 (tl): Shutterstock / Jun Mu; P161 (cl): Getty Images / View Pictures; P161 (bl): Getty Images / Black 100; P161 (br): Shutterstock / Claudio Zaccherini; P162 (tr): Shutterstock / Sean Pavone; P162 (cl): Shutterstock / Sergii Rudiuk; P163 (bl): Shutterstock / feiyuezhangjie; P163 (b): Shutterstock / Hung Chung Chi; P163 (br): Shutterstock / Ben Bryant; P164 (tr): Getty Images / ChinaFotoPress; P165 (c): Shutterstock / shahreen; P166 (cl): Shutterstock / beyolsan; P166 (cr): Artist: Artist Cao Chong-en / Shutterstock / mary416; P166 (br): Shutterstock / Everything; P167 (t): Getty Images / Maria Swärd; P167 (bl): Shutterstock / saiko3p; Pages 168–169 (t): Shutterstock / Peera_stockfoto; P168 (tr): Shutterstock / Etakundoy; P168 (cl): Shutterstock / 1000 Words; P169 (cl): Alamy / David Ball; P169 (b): Shutterstock / nimon; P170 (tr): Getty / catchlights_sg; P170 (br): Getty Images / fiftymm99; P171 (tl): Shutterstock / nattanan726; P171 (c): Getty Images / Wilfred Y. Wong; P172 (c): Shutterstock / Jimmy Tran; P172 (b): Shutterstock / John Bill; P173 (tr): Alamy / dbimages; P173 (cl): Getty Images / Lonely Planet; P173 (b): Shutterstock / suronin; Pages 174–175 (t): Getty Images / UIG; P174 (cl): Shutterstock / donsimon; P174 (b): Shutterstock / saiko3p; P175 (bl): Shutterstock / Allen. G; P176 (tr): Shutterstock / Sean Pavone; P176 (cr): Alamy / Jeremy Sutton-Hibbert; P176 (bl): Shutterstock / jiratto; P177 (b): Shutterstock / J. Henning Buchholz; Pages 178–179 (t): Shutterstock / Luciano Mortula; P178 (tc): Shutterstock / Wiennat M; P178 (cl): Alamy / Aflo Co. Ltd.; P178 (br): Getty Images / Yoshikazu Tsuno; P179 (c): Shutterstock / Sean Pavone; P180 (tr): Shutterstock / Sean Pavone; P180 (c): Alamy / Amana Images Inc.; P180 (br): Shutterstock / marcociannarel; P181 (tr): Shutterstock / BigGabig; P181 (c): Alamy / Sean Pavone; P181 (bl): Shutterstock / Travel Stock; P182 (cr): Getty Images / Alex Linghorn; Pages 182–183 (c): Getty Images / Nick Ledger; P183 (tl): Alamy / ITAR-TASS Photo Agency; P183 (cl): Shutterstock / Thanthima Lim; P183 (b): Alamy / Eric Lafforgue; P184 (cr): Shutterstock / Freedom Man; P184 (bl); Shutterstock / Takashi Images; P185 (tl): Shutterstock / Sean Pavone; P185 (cr): Shutterstock / PKphotograph; P186 (tr): Getty Images / Keystone; P186 (cl): Getty Images / John Borthwick; P186 (bc): Shutterstock / AlexanderZam; P187 (t): Getty Images / Louise Denton Photography; P188 (tr): Shutterstock / Lorimer Images; P188 (bl): Alamy / Michael Willis; P189 (tr): Shutterstock / Nokuro; P189 (bl): Shutterstock / Kaneos Media; P190 (tr): Shutterstock / Lee Torrens; Pages 190–191 (c): Shutterstock / MagSpace; P191 (tr): Alamy / The Print Collector; P191 (b): Shutterstock / Nils Versemann; P192 (tr): Shutterstock / Nils Versemann; P192 (bl): Alamy / EPA; Pages 192–193 (b): Shutterstock / Neale Cousland; P193 (tr): Getty Images / Quinn Rooney; P194 (c): Alamy / Greg Balfour Evans; P194 (b): Shutterstock / my-summit; P195 (cl): Getty Images / Robin Smith; P195 (cr): Getty Images / Thien Do; P195 (br): Shutterstock / PominOz; P196 (cr): Shutterstock / Phillip Minnis; P196 (bl): artwork creation by Danny Rose for Vivid Sydney Festival Getty Images / Krzysztof Dydynski; P197 (t): Corbis / John Carnemolla; P197 (b): Getty Images / Mike Hewitt; P198 (bl): Alamy / Aroon Thaewchatturat; P198 (br): Alamy / John Arnold Images; P199 (cl): Alamy / travellinglight; P199 (r): Shutterstock / Sam DCruz; Pages 200–201 (t): Shutterstock / Pichugin Dmitry; P200 (cl): Alamy / National Geographic Creative; P201 (cl): Getty Images / Adina Tovy; P201 (bc): Alamy / Dan Santillo NZ; P202 (cr): Alamy / age fotostock; P203 (t): Shutterstock / Naruedom Yaempongsa; P203 (cr): Getty Images / Cameron Spencer; P203 (bl): Alamy / AF archive; Pages 204–205 (t): Alamy / David Wall; P204 (cl): Shutterstock / MJ Prototype; P205 (r): Alamy / Tribaleye Images / J. Marshall; P205 (cl): Getty Images / Werner Forman; Pages 206–207 (t): Alamy / Atmotu Images; P206 (cl): Alamy / Niday Picture Library; P207 (cr): Alamy / Antiques & Collectables; P207 (bl): Shutterstock / Minerva Studio; Pages 208–209 (c) Getty Images / Jonas Gratzer; P208 (bl): Alamy / David Glassey; P209 (tr): Getty Images / Time Life Pictures.